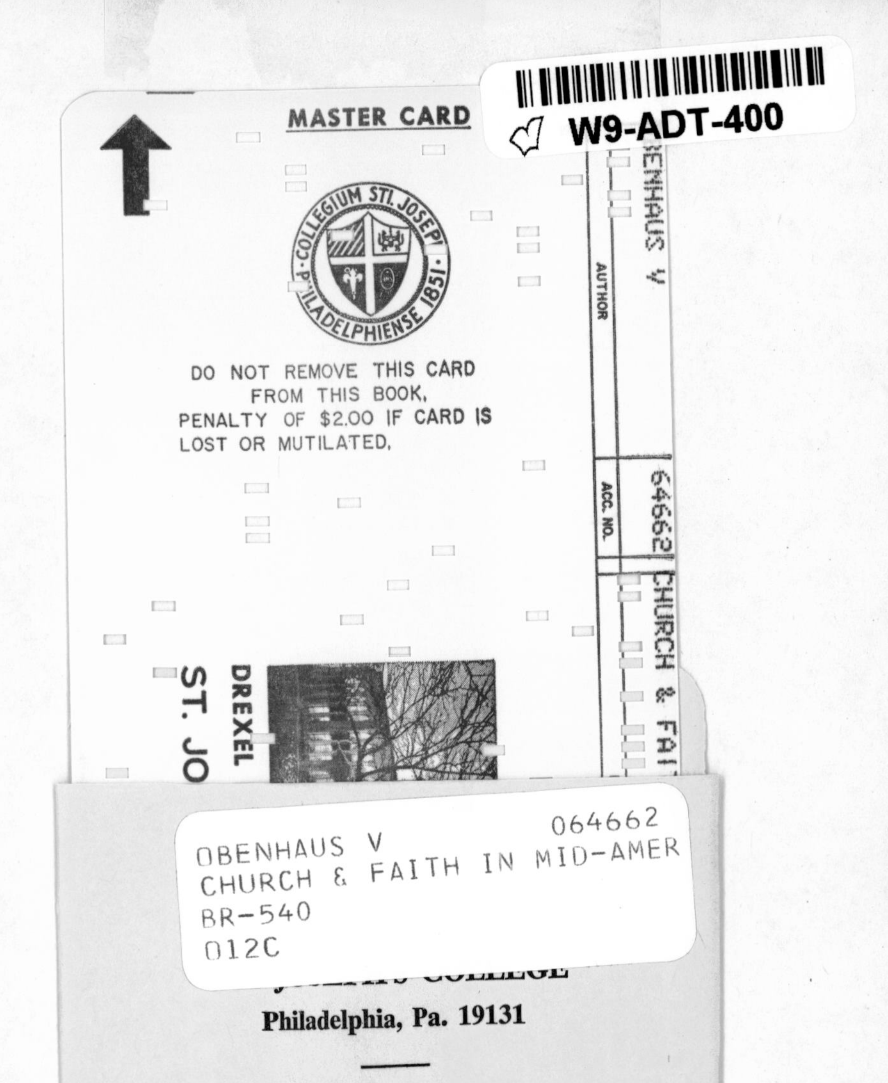

OBENHAUS V 064662
CHURCH & FAITH IN MID-AMER
BR-540
012C

JOSEPH'S COLLEGE
Philadelphia, Pa. 19131

---

1. Books may be kept two weeks and may be renewed once for the same period, except 7 day books and magazines.

2. A fine of two cents a day will be charged on each book which is not returned according to the above rule. No book will be issued to any person incurring such a fine until it has been paid.

3. All injuries to books, beyond reasonable wear, and all losses shall be made good to the satisfaction of the Librarian.

4. Each borrower is held responsible for all books drawn on his card and for all fines accruing on the same.

DEMCO

THE CHURCH AND FAITH IN MID-AMERICA

THE CHURCH AND FAITH IN MID-AMERICA

by VICTOR OBENHAUS

BR540
O12C

64662

THE WESTMINSTER PRESS
PHILADELPHIA

Copyright © MCMLXIII W. L. Jenkins

All rights reserved—no part of this book may be reproduced in any form without permission in writing from the publisher, except by a reviewer who wishes to quote brief passages in connection with a review in magazine or newspaper.

Library of Congress Catalog Card No. 62-13873

PRINTED IN THE UNITED STATES OF AMERICA

To my New England born wife,
who has also come to love the prairie

CONTENTS

LIST OF TABLES

PREFACE

IN OUR NATIONAL LIFE we have come to accept the fact that a common culture has been evolving. Technology, with its impact through media of communication, the common school, use of similar mechanical devices, accessibility to the same products of manufacture, and industrial mobility—to mention only a few of its manifestations—has contributed to this cultural uniformity. With most other aspects of life thus influenced, it would be strange if religious beliefs and practices were not also affected. Discerning the range of differences and the measure of uniformity expressed by individuals subjected to these forces constitutes one of the purposes of this analysis.

American religious life is fostered by a multitude of denominations, each theoretically possessing distinctive characteristics. Though original reasons for their separateness may have become blurred or may even have disappeared, each denomination attempts to assert its justification for existence and to expand its activities and membership. Originally unique purposes and beliefs gave justification for the denomination's role.

It was, therefore, a further purpose of this study to determine whether these various denominations are currently influencing their adherents in a manner consistent with implied traditions of internal and external authority.

A commonly accepted index of religious vitality is the degree of ethical responsibility exhibited. To that end, the religious beliefs of the adherents to the various denominations now active in the geographic area studied were correlated with their attitudes toward prominent social issues.

One county, designated "Corn County" in this study, deemed typical of the Midwest, exclusive of metropolitan centers, was selected for the study. Demographic and attitudinal data were secured by interviewing a random sample of approximately twelve hundred individuals, taken from (1) a county seat town, (2) an agricultural service center, (3) an industrial town, and (4) two open-country townships.

No attempt has been made to "prove" that the findings of this study are equally applicable to other areas of the nation or even of the Midwest. Neither can it be insisted that they represent the religious attitudes of metropolitan residents. Presentation of the study's findings to persons in other parts of the nation and to metropolitan residents have elicited almost uniform response, however—namely, that the results would not differ greatly if a similar study was made in other types of areas. We would prefer to leave to the reader any judgment both as to the relevance of these findings to his area of residence and to the implications for personal and institutional religious life.

V. O.

ACKNOWLEDGMENTS

A LONG AND DISTINGUISHED TRADITION of concern for the social manifestations of religion and for research in religious life has characterized Chicago Theological Seminary. The author, and those associated with him in this study of an area typical of the Midwest, were drawn to that seminary in part because of this tradition. Throughout the five years during which the research was conducted, immeasurable support in both time and money have been supplied by this seminary. While the Federated Theological Faculty of the University of Chicago was in existence, funds to support a graduate student each year were provided from its research budget. The first substantial grant, aside from grants of the institutions sponsoring the study, came from the Board of Home Missions of the Congregational Christian Churches. The Sears-Roebuck Foundation made possible the continuation of the study in its early period by a generous grant. In "Main Town" of "Corn County," the Ministers Association early saw the implications of the study and made a helpful contribution. From the Board of National Missions of The United Presbyterian Church in the U.S.A. and the Farm

Foundation came funds sufficient to employ a graduate student interviewer for a summer. To the New World Foundation we are especially indebted for the fact that its staff saw the significance of the type of research being conducted and made available funds in sufficient amount to bring the study to completion.

In attempting to recognize all of those who have been helpful in such an undertaking, it is, of course, impossible to single out every individual who made a contribution. Fellow faculty members and students in seminars have given counsel and criticisms. Dr. Samuel C. Kincheloe, a former colleague, contributed much in the planning stages of the research. Charles England served as interviewer and later as field supervisor. Donna England (Mrs. Charles) was, likewise, an interviewer. In a similar capacity, Mr. and Mrs. Richard Rautio, Mr. and Mrs. Ronald Hutchinson, Howard Russell and Jackson Campbell, participated in varying lengths of time. Mrs. Gisele Mendel provided the analyses for the Thematic Apperception Tests. Constance Obenhaus assisted in coding the interviews. Mrs. Frances Ritsch contributed immeasurably in perceptive counsel, in meticulous attention to details of the study and in patient preparation of the manuscript.

More than to any other person, however, the author is indebted to his former student and now colleague, Dr. W. Widick Schroeder. Without his wisdom and skill this study would not have been conducted.

V. O.

CHAPTER I

RELIGION AND A TYPICAL MIDWEST COUNTY

A CAREFUL LOOK into the religious life of a typical corn belt county will probably reveal a picture very similar to, if not actually identical with, what could be found in many other counties of this region. More or less officially, the corn belt is composed of some 469 counties, and in popular opinion it is the heart of the American Midwest. The county chosen for the intensive gaze qualifies in being at least as representative of the total corn belt as any other, based upon a comparison with the three typical corn belt counties designated by the United States Department of Agriculture (Henry County, Indiana; Hamilton County, Iowa; Seward County, Nebraska).

Some analysts of American society, among them Graham Hutton, author of *Midwest at Noon* (University of Chicago Press, 1945), contend that the Midwest and its corn belt may be the area most truly representative of American life. This exceeds any judgment we could make. It does perhaps justify a conclusion that the Midwest is not atypical of the nation and that some characteristics reflected in it may have their parallels in other parts of the country as well.

The ultimate purpose of the portrayal is not primarily to describe the full range of religious life in the Midwest. It is, rather, to ascertain what is happening to religious life and thought, especially as these are influenced both by the institutional life of the church and by other forces that are affecting our culture.

Religious beliefs and their consequent expression in action have always been influenced by the culture in which that particular religion is practiced. At the same time, religion influences the culture of society. This, however, is a theoretical, a theological, and a philosophical problem with which it is not our purpose to deal here. More will be said of this after some of the findings of the study have been portrayed.

Though Corn County is primarily oriented toward agriculture, it is also representative of the corn belt in the increasing number of small factories locating in it. Thus influential in determining the life and thought of Corn County people is the impact of the peculiar combination of agriculture and industry which conditions the total life of the corn belt.

The uniquely favored position of this region resulting from climate, soil, and water resources has attracted to it the population which in turn contributed human resources. Its farm population has "the highest and evenest level of living among farm families in the nation." (Carl C. Taylor and others, *Rural Life in the United States;* Alfred A. Knopf, 1949.) Educational attainment levels are commensurate with the levels of living. In church membership and participation it is probably unsurpassed.

No area of the nation has adopted the contributions of science in both plant and animal life and in technology more readily than the corn belt. Not only does the high degree of farm mechanization require mechanical skill but also the ability to pay for the machines necessary to save manual labor. Its people possess the education to cope with and accelerate a technological society; this in turn implies competence in the market place. All these factors combine to suggest that the people of Corn County are subject to the influences affecting an agricultural area that has appropriated the most recent advances in commerce and technology.

The largest percentage of the population of the corn belt, however, is not involved in agriculture—great cities are within its boundaries and many more on its periphery. Chicago, Omaha, Des Moines, Indianapolis, Peoria, and others are fully within its boundaries, while such metropolitan areas as Kansas City, St. Louis, Minneapolis–St. Paul, and even Detroit, have a profound influence on the region by virtue of their proximity to it. At least fifty-five cities in the region have more than fifty thousand population.

The industrial life that characterizes the metropolis is no longer confined to the large urban centers. Rare is the small city, for example, that has not in recent years welcomed at least one factory. Rarer still is the community that is not seeking an industry to locate in or near its corporate limits. Agriculture and industry are becoming increasingly synchronized in the corn belt. The mind of the people living within its borders has long been conditioned by the life of the metropolitan centers and the technological developments which have influenced every conceivable phase of the region's life. In this respect it is no different from other regions of the nation except perhaps that the process has gone forward more rapidly here than in many other areas of the United States.

It is in this situation that the church, as the instrument of religious life, seeks to perform its ministry. In the next chapter we shall describe the particular county chosen for this study and tell something of the religious institutions that perform their functions within it. It suffices here to suggest that the church as an institution attempts to fulfill its ministry in an area in which the mind of its people has been powerfully shaped by the developments of science and technology which have revolutionized agriculture and given the predominance to industry in our national life. This process has been so thoroughly documented by countless other studies that it need not be repeated here. A few manifestations of this impact of technological development will suffice. For example, the uniformity of speech and dress brought about both by the communications media affecting everyone who can read or listen is widely apparent, but nowhere more vividly than among young people of high school age. At the same time it must be said that not all the impact is in one direction. One notes the willingness of urban youth to wear jeans and Levi's, the traditional garb of rural youth. Aside from the economy and convenience factors, it is significant that this garb no longer carries the stigma of "hick" or "hayseed." Future Farmers of America and 4-H and the favored position of some portions of agriculture have elevated farm youth to a position of esteem and perhaps even of envy.

Prominent in the rapidly changing rural life are the new leisure-time activities and interests for women and the heightened commercial and scientific interests of men.

It is commonplace in these times to accept the fact that rural women are no longer slaves to kitchen and farm duties. The proliferation of bridge clubs, flower-arranging sessions, home-decorating courses, and style shows is as much a part of rural life as of urban. When the local banker or Federal Reserve specialist addresses farmers on credit or when the state agricultural college authority speaks on antibiotics or land tenure arrangements or innovations in agricultural machinery, a full house is assured. The fact is that farming has become a business inseparably tied to urban markets and the centers of technology and science.

This is not to say that farming is only a business. The Homestead Act of 1862 merely popularized and made formal what was already an established part of American agricultural policy—the family farm. It sought to guarantee the preservation of individual and societal values which stem from this historic pattern of American rural life. In fact, it is the conflict between the historic values associated with the family established on its own farmstead and the business-commercial aspects of agriculture which constitute the focus of the present dilemma in our agricultural policy. As a nation we are torn between two major loyalties: (1) the desire to preserve the family farm which has symbolized our national roots, and (2) our pride in technological and commercial progress. This conflict is exemplified in the concept of parity, our desire to give to the farmer a buying power commensurate with his investment in his farm plant and the amount of labor he must expend.

"Agri-business" is the appropriate and meaningful term that has come to characterize agriculture in an area so favored as the corn belt. But the fact that farming in the history of this nation is regarded as something more than a business has contributed to the dilemma. It has come to symbolize moral values as well as economics. Consciously or unconsciously, religion and agriculture are regarded as inseparably related. Just as a state of harmony between religion and economics has been the objective of long and diligent search, so in the corn belt (as well as in much of the rest of America) the role of religion in a culture dominated by "agri-business" constitutes a serious dilemma for the primary instrument of religion—the church.

CHURCH AND THE CHURCHES

The term "church" is used here in its sociological sense rather than its theological, ecclesiological, or supernatural sense. Whatever else the church is, it is also manifest in recognizable local groups of people, each having been assembled or gathered for avowed purposes. It is, therefore, these groups and their buildings and organizations which constitute a substantial phase of the life of the church. These organizations may go by different names, and presumably there is something that differentiates one group from another in its beliefs, its way of worship. The latter, in turn, stems from the church's beliefs and its type of government. Obviously, many individuals take these implied differences quite seriously. Some join a particular church in order to accentuate the difference between their beliefs and those of another denomination. Also, differences in national backgrounds, economic and educational levels, determine membership for some people, while business or social advantages are determinative for others.

In what is designated as an open society in the United States, the movement in and out of class designations constitutes a source of national pride. It has its parallels in the movement of individuals from one church to another, something that was not possible for those who had only the choice of a national church in the countries from which they came. This freedom of movement between churches and the basis for church selection constitutes one of the phenomena that strongly attracted the authors of this study. The Midwest corn belt is characterized by a broad range of denominations. No one or two overshadow the others, as may be true in some other portions of the country. Again, it seemed that some well-defined changes were occurring. For example, a generation or more ago, persons who were moving up the ladder of economic stability sought to affiliate with particular churches. Or again, because of marriage, business connections, or place of work, it seemed advisable to become identified with a particular denomination. Today there seems to be a change in the respective positions of some denominations. Some that were on the dismissing side of the ledger earlier are now on the receiving side. This is one of the hypotheses it seemed wise to explore.

Certain churches spend a large amount of time and energy in Biblical instruction and in education along lines of denominational loyalty and emphasis. Does this make their communicants any more sensitive to the major issues of our times and more desirous of reasserting the historic values of their faith in relation to these problems? Are they different in any way from those persons who engage in markedly variant types of church activity and who spend little time studying doctrines and learning creeds? There has long been a suspicion that other forces were more influential than the churches in shaping our society and that other than theological and creedal factors were perhaps more determinative.

Still another observation that needed to be examined arises from the situation where churches may be serving purposes quite separate from, and possibly alien to, the avowed nature of the church itself. For example, one of the consequences of the church's life may be the fracturing rather than the unifying of the community. If this is true, may it be that some other agency has replaced the church as the instrument making for unity and harmony in the community? Obviously, these organizations that are known locally as "churches" serve some necessary function or they would not survive. Actually, some of them are surviving very well, judging from their appearances. They are frequently well painted, with landscaped grounds, possessing attractive modern parsonages, manses, or rectories; the older churches may often be remodeled, incorporating a chancel, electric organ, and dossal hangings. New churches reflect imaginative architecture and, in keeping with the rising economic level of their parishioners, attain an appearance of stability which stone and an imaginative architect can provide. All of this money poured into the physical plant must signify something by way of interest in the usefulness and the perpetuation of the institution.

To this evidence of financial well-being must also be added the fact that members supporting these churches seem to be willing to provide for the support of a hired leader or perhaps several leaders and their families. Funds are available for the maintenance of staff and physical properties. These are frequently regarded as the *church.* A closer look at the economic structure of many of these local churches, however, would raise doubts as to the seriousness of the members' acceptance of their relationship to a church larger in scope than their local unit. Obviously, many church members related to small churches would prefer to hire leadership at a very modest and perhaps restricting salary than to join with others in developing a church of sufficient scope to be able to pay an adequate salary and provide a fuller range of opportunity for young and old. The limited size of the local organization seems to provide something more important than a wider array of church activities might afford in a consolidation with other small units.

Despite the proliferation and division of religious organizations, most of the people living in a small town or in the common area of a larger town attend the same school activities and relate to each other in clubs and community organizations. Is there, then, something deeply meaningful deriving from their church affiliation? Does *denomination* provide something essential in a society that is becoming highly standardized through the school and other organizations to which individuals belong irrespective of denomination?

Americans take it for granted that religious values saturate their national life. Are they not written into our most important documents? Recently we added the words "under God" to our spoken salute to the flag to reinforce our protests of religious devotion. The Mayflower Compact, the Declaration of Independence, and the Preamble to the Constitution announce our devotion to, and dependence on, the Creator. Forty-two state constitutions acknowledge the supremacy of God. Oaths of public office and veracity in the courts are posited on the religious foundations of the nation. Basically, then, it is assumed that our national life takes its direction from this loyalty to the God of whose existence and work the Bible testifies.

The primary work of the church is, presumably, to clarify man's relationship to God and to help him experience fully what this means. The work of the churches, then, must be judged in the light of this fundamental purpose—all else is incidental—that is, if we take seriously the fact that the church has one primary function.

There has never been an accurate religious census in the United States. Roughly it has been estimated that something less than 2 per cent of Americans disavow the existence of a Supreme Being and that approximately 65 per cent of the American people are related to some religious organization. Figures for regions of the nation are not accurately available, but the number of churches and a rough estimate of the measure of participation in them on the part of people in the corn belt would indicate that the church population in that region is at least as high as the national average. From these observations it can well be deduced that religious life is expected to influence strongly the total ways of life of those who live in this particular region, the corn belt.

If it is true that religion is so influential in the lives of these people, we have reason to be concerned with what religion means to them. In addition to the fact that the church buildings are well maintained, every community has a corps of paid religious leaders, musical specialists, and custodians of property.

Assessments made by denominational headquarters are assumed with varying enthusiasm but they are, for the most part, accepted because of the assumption that the total work of the denomination must be supported. For the majority of church people in the corn belt, the message or content of their religion is not dictated by outside agencies or authorities. Their religious leaders are employed in accordance with some criteria which they have established for themselves or which have been suggested to them. What is it that the people of these churches wish to perpetuate? What values do they assume are being preserved? What function do they assume their church organization is fulfilling? Without anticipating the findings of the study, it will probably come as no surprise that very few church or nonchurch people have seemingly given much thought to these questions. Apparently religion in its social manifestation and in the organized life of churches simply *is*, and it is the function of the churches to foster this.

SOME HYPOTHESES

In a time when more attention is being paid by seminaries, denominational leaders, and interdenominational agencies to the question of the nature of the church than to anything else in the entire realm of religious discussion, the local church often seems quite unaware of this concern. But the nature of the church and the faith that determines it have implications for the relationship of the local church to the community, to other religious organizations, and to its own people. It seemed to those undertaking this study that there was an apparent irrelevance between much of what was happening in the churches and the main issues with which society at large was dealing. If this was true, then the common assumption that the church was responsible for the basic values in our society was either untenable or its significance was unknown. This obviously raises the question of the church's own presuppositions and those which its people have been taking for granted. They do not seem to be the same. Are other forces establishing and sustaining the values that Americans in general espouse and that are so commonly accepted in the Midwest? If so, what are these stronger influences, and how do their values coincide with the values inherent in the Christian faith and the institutions supporting and promoting that faith?

For persons to whom the church is more than a holding

operation, it is a source of regret to see it often become principally a place of refuge or a tool to sustain the values and standards dictated by agencies other than the church. The priestly and prophetic functions have rarely found expression in the same individual or institution. Nevertheless, it is assumed that in the light of its history and the requirements placed upon it by its faith, the church is the bearer of both the priestly and the prophetic note. Rarely, however, are the two to be found in a single company of God's people. Times of strain and anxiety encourage the priestly emphasis. Stability becomes important. Inevitably, individuals turn to the organizations or movements that provide security in turbulent times. Here the priestly function of the church serves an unmistakable need. But by the same token, the very uncertainties and tendencies to cling to doubtful resources may serve to inhibit the very prophetic emphasis that might give leadership or help in moving out of the turbulence. A rather casual and unsystematic appraisal of religious life in the geographic area studied, based on personal contacts with church people and religious leaders, would seem to reveal few evidences of prophetic interest on the part of the church as an institution either in Corn County or in the area surrounding it.

CHURCH-COMMUNITY RELATIONSHIPS

Whether, therefore, the church is fulfilling its dual mission of priestly and prophetic function constitutes one of the principal concerns of this study. There was a strong suspicion that many, if not most, of the church people of this region had not come to grips with the fuller intent or purpose of the church. Who was responsible for this, it would be difficult to decide; but that there seemed to be a deficiency was commonly agreed. For example, in the county ultimately chosen for intensive analysis, the tentacles of a crime syndicate had moved into many channels of the county's life. Corruption, later fully documented, had saturated the state's attorney's office and the police. Vice and gambling were wide open, and all this was common knowledge. Yet none of the churches or church people felt impelled to take any steps to counteract this disintegration. Parenthetically it can be stated that some alert ministers and aroused laymen of their congregations did tackle this problem and ultimately broke open a state-wide scandal. The churches had declined to confront the issue because they lacked any strong sense of obligation for the problem and because it would have brought into the open the friction between rival wings of the same party. Political peace was more important than civic decency.

This political scandal is possibly the most dramatic illustration of the church's aloofness from the real life within which it is set. It is, however, by no means the most significant example of the irrelevance or confusion of organized religious life. The fracturing of religious expression into numerous separate units or local churches has reduced any sense of total responsibility for the community—perhaps on the theory of what is everybody's business is nobody's business. The decisions affecting the quality of community life have been left to agencies other than the church, notably the school and the political organizations of the communities. What, if any, were the obligations deriving from their church affiliations which the city fathers and the board of education members maintain? Evidence points to the fact that little thought had been given to so fundamental a problem—fundamental because in the tradition of some of the most prominent churches their very theology calls for a community responsibility inseparably related to the life of the church.

That there are marked differences in the tradition and historic background of many of the churches in this area is obvious. Ethnic groups that moved into the corn belt brought with them their theories and traditions of church community life. The New England Yankees who arrived first took it for granted that the standards of Protestant church life that they had known or that had been experienced under an established church in New England would guarantee righteousness in the new prairie life of the Midwest. Immigrants coming with other religious and civic traditions soon challenged this assumption, but they were nonetheless concerned with individual righteousness. The kind of church-state traditions out of which many of them had come did not prepare them for a sense of community responsibility. Uniformity of culture was shattered, but the impact of individual integrity based on Biblical foundations was still profoundly to be felt throughout the area. A personal ethic could be assumed; that it would result in collective action in a common attack on the mass forces of evil could not be so readily expected.

The diminishing sense of responsibility for total community life could not be laid wholly at the door of the division among the churches. Undoubtedly this had something to do with it, both because of the absence of unity and because of the proliferation of interests which made necessary the emergence of still other organizations to deal with the total concerns of the community. Still larger and more powerful forces were at work. An expanding economy and a seemingly limitless future, based upon both hard work and good luck in real estate acquisitions in farms and cities, inevitably shifted the attention to the problems of personal gain. America in this period of its greatest westward expansion was heavily influenced by what is generally known as "the gospel of wealth." It encouraged individuals to believe that in some way their personal gain was to be equated with religious virtue. The virtue of industry and frugality became an inseparable part of religious life. Even the hymns most commonly sung reflected this motif. "Work, for the Night Is Coming" typifies a whole era of hymn production.

While religious life fostered concern with personal virtues, commercial and industrial life was beginning to take on the pattern of vastness which has now become the standard and expected form of industrial society. Little if anything in the life of the churches in the predominantly rural areas, and presumably this is true of the urban areas as well, trained them to sense any responsibility on the part of church people for the societal values that were being altered or created by the very pattern of bigness. In the face of the emergence of great combinations in ownership and management of business, of communications, notably the newspapers, and subsequently of labor, the churches in their proliferation of small units could offer little more than a refuge and a haven of security in small-group life. It is not surprising, therefore, that church participants, as it is subsequently revealed, knew nothing of the attempt of their denomination or of groups of denominations to confront the vast movements in a society of large combinations—industry, communications, politics—with the witness of the Christian message as it seems to speak to the total human scene.

In the local community with the individual churches decreasingly able to make an effective witness based upon a fundamental knowledge of both the priestly and prophetic tradition to which they belong, it is not difficult to understand why, in most communities, if not all, there have emerged organizations that transcend denominational lines and provide an actual unity which the apparently dubious theoretical unity of the church cannot provide. It is understandable that these newer unifying organizations—the public school, the farm organization, the political organization—become the reliable and accepted spokesmen for community values.

These are the hypotheses or suppositions that come to the fore as a result of increasing familiarity with Corn County and the corn belt which it symbolizes.

CHAPTER II

CORN COUNTY

FROM THE TIME the tourist enters Corn County from the east until he leaves its boundaries some forty-five miles farther westward, he finds little to distinguish it from most of the other 468 counties in the corn belt. Whether traveling on one of the two national transcontinental highways or on any of the less-traveled blacktop or gravel roads, he knows he is in the corn belt. The most prominent vegetation is the plant that the newcomer to American shores received from the Indian, and that, for reasons of climate, geography, markets, and transportation facilities, has achieved its heaviest production in the Midwest—corn. However, the prosperous, well-kept farms which beget admiration do not derive their principal income from the sale of the grain. Rather, it is converted into much more profitable products, namely, steaks and bacon.

Cattle and hogs are the principal business of Corn County and the source of its greatest wealth.* Many radio sets are

* Crops and livestock values, Corn County, 1959:
(1) Cattle—$16,667,000.00
(2) Hogs—$9,401,800.00

tuned in each day to the report from the stockyards indicating the principal sellers of cattle and hogs, and almost every day one stock feeder from Corn County is singled out for mention. Farm and livestock journals are scanned to ascertain the corn-hog ratio, i.e., the cost of the number of bushels of corn required to pay for one hundred pounds of pork. Aside from a few events in its early history, including an Indian massacre and the exploits of a famous preacher-politician, Corn County is best known for its principal products—cattle and hogs—and the land values determined by the prices of those animals.

But Corn County is not wholly agricultural, and this contributes to its typicality for the Midwest. In the two largest towns of the county, each approximately six thousand in population, industry has been or is becoming increasingly influential. This study is, in a large measure, concerned with the consequences of this industrialization, and its parallel technological advance in agriculture, for religious life.

RIVER TOWN

A principal river of the state provides a small piece of the county's boundary. In a city on that river and adjacent to Corn County is located a widely known precision industry. Close to this industrial city, and actually in Corn County, is a town in which live many of the workers in that industry. More important, though, than the fact that skilled workers are there is the history of the town itself, which for purposes of this study we shall call River Town. Originally

(3) All livestock—$26,679,700.00
(4) Corn—$18,751,000.00
(5) All crops—$25,606,900.00
(6) Acreage, principal crops—387,800
Source: U.S. Crop Reporting Service

it was made notable as a mining center and as the place of the founding of the United Mine Workers of America. Today the mines are all closed, but in every direction are vivid reminders in the form of the slag piles which were still in formation up to the time of the First World War. Descendants of those miners, as well as some of the original workers in the mines, now make River Town their community.

Four Roman Catholic Churches, each with a different ethnic background, and one Congregational Church, founded by Welsh miners, attest to the origins of the people who gave River Town its original flavor. The presence of some twenty-three saloons in a four-block area, the repeated raids on gambling joints, and the concentration of crime leadership in this community likewise reflect the influence of the past. From 1910 until 1950 the largest immigrant group settling in Corn County came from Italy and concentrated their residence in River Town. The industries of the adjacent cities as well as the mining around this community attracted the Italians. This, plus the arrival of Lithuanians and Poles for similar work opportunities, explains the predominance of Roman Catholics in River Town.

This much attention has been paid to River Town because it is regarded as atypical of the rest of the county. Because of its size, approximately equal to that of the county seat, it exercises considerable political power, heightened by the presence of those who seek protection for their extralegal activities. Despite the fact that it is different from the rest of the county, its presence can never be discounted. For that reason it has been included for special consideration along with several other communities in the study.

River Town is not the only community to entertain industrial activity in an otherwise largely agricultural county. Two other communities are marked by important industrial activity. Along the river mentioned previously is a one-industry town, the residents and employees being dominantly of Italian birth or descent. This community was not specifically included in the study because it was believed that River Town was sufficiently representative of both to be used for the sample.

MAIN TOWN

The other community with substantial industrial activity is the county seat town, which we shall call "Main Town." It has experienced what has become increasingly the standard pattern for county seat towns, the concentration of government activity, schools, farm organizations, banking, and, to some extent, church life. Fifty years ago, those who were deeply concerned with the fate of the country church were beginning to speak of "the killing range of the county seat church." With attention already drawn toward the county seat for many services and functions, it was logical that its churches should increase in strength, and in so doing they—for the most part unintentionally—depleted the strength of churches of their own denomination in neighboring towns and open country.

With so much of the organizational life and leadership concentrating in the county seat town, it was thought probable that this community would reflect advanced thinking in many areas. Since the leadership was scattered throughout all the churches, though in varying degrees, the response from church members of Main Town would presumably reflect the benefits accruing to Main Town churches.

Today two national highways converge in Main Town.

Both eventually lead to Chicago, for generations the packing house and farm marketing capital of the Midwest. Ease of access to marketing facilities serves to highlight the typicality of Corn County and points to its desirability as both a farming and a residence area. Likewise, two of the great railroads running from Chicago to the West Coast pass through Corn County—in fact, they cross each other just west of Main Town. Thus, in addition to splendid highway facilities the county possesses excellent rail services east and west.

With the dispersal of industrial plants and the search for a stable and perhaps less expensive labor force, new factories are to be found in all the "Main Towns" of the Midwest. Four such factories with, for the most part, new buildings and new managerial personnel and labor have located in Main Town within recent years. A busy chamber of commerce now promises still others in the very near future. For many years an introduction of new industry was discouraged, the local people knowing full well that the arrival of factory workers might change the tone and raise the school tax rate of this beautiful and primarily residential community. But with school costs rising, the possibilities of assistance in the tax returns and the likelihood of increased business on Main Street have increased the importance of industrial expansion, and its opponents have become a minority.

MIGRATIONS AND DENOMINATIONS

The arrival of an industrial labor force confronts Corn County and its Main Town with a sixth major immigration. The other five have left varying impacts since the first pioneers came out from New England in 1823. It would be impossible to understand the psychology of Corn County and the changes that have occurred in the past century and a quarter, without an appreciation of the contributions of these migrations. A brief description of them is given in the following paragraphs.

In 1830 Corn County was still a wilderness traversed only by Indians. Even the city of Chicago was three years short of its establishment as a permanent community. But in Massachusetts, a company of people had formed a colony and were preparing to transport themselves and their goods to the rich upland prairie about which advance agents had written in glowing terms.

For reasons that today make strange reading, the people of the eastern seaboard had previously been discouraged from westward migration largely from fear of the loss of political power to the commercial segment of the eastern population. When it became apparent that the eastern seaboard could no longer contain all the people who wanted to live in that part of the nation, or provide an adequate basis for their living, the forces that restricted westward movement were relaxed. These New England migrants were often themselves skilled craftsmen and merchants. However, the possibility of cheap land and the excitement of opening the frontier encouraged them to undertake a wholly new kind of living.

It is one of the phenomena of American history that a yeoman class has never arisen in American agriculture. Presumably, developments have occurred so rapidly both in the type of agriculture and in the financial and commercial aspects of farming that a stable class doing the same thing their forefathers had done never had opportunity to form.

The New England Yankees who poured into the corn belt

had known a common culture. They came out of regions influenced by common forces for a century and a half. A similar type of government prevailed in all the communities from which they came, and a more or less common theological foundation characterized the church life of their religious institutions.

Originally Corn County land was purchased largely by migrants from New England. Much of it had been sold in plots described in attractive literature and many who purchased land didn't bother to go to the area where they held title. Those who did actually make the move, however, often bought up the holdings of those who had originally made purchases. Thus in early stages of the settlement of the county, New England Yankees both owned and farmed the new prairie land they had acquired. They established the same kind of churches they had known in their native New England—Baptist, Congregational, and Episcopalian. Because they believed in education, they established schools beyond the common school level, and when their offspring completed those requirements they sent them off to college, with the result that that became almost standard for the area—the young people did not return to the farm. Business and the professions throughout the nation have been inestimably enhanced by the children and grandchildren of the first migration to Corn County and the Midwest—the New England Yankee.

The potato famine in Ireland and the continent-wide outburst of revolutions in Europe in 1848 synchronized with the development of the railroad in America and the opening of the vast public domain. In all, forty million immigrants have come to these shores, millions of them settling in the Midwest and its corn belt. Most of those who remained in the rural portion of the Midwest came from Germany and the Scandinavian countries. Those who remained in the metropolitan centers came from southern Europe and Russia. Swedish immigrants chose to follow one of the main rail lines west of Chicago and began to colonize substantially in Corn County and immediately west thereof. Interestingly, the Norwegians seemed to follow the other main rail line and colonized, though not so extensively, in the towns through which it passed. This Scandinavian colonization has substantial significance for the study of contemporary religious life in Corn County. They came with only a will to work and are today fully represented in all the major occupations and positions.

The first contingent of Irish came with the building of the railroads and later to serve as farm hands. The presence of Roman Catholic churches in many of the towns of Corn County attests to the presence of the Irish immigrant who came to work on the land and remained to till it as full partner. Attending public school together, Protestants and Catholics found their mates and seemingly moved with equal ease amidst companions in the spouse's faith. To anticipate the findings of the study briefly it can be asserted that the ecclesiastical differences have often wilted before friendship patterns and common community concerns.

Not as large numerically, but of far-reaching significance for the life of Corn County has been the German migration in the persons of Mennonite immigrants and German Lutherans. As was true of the earlier Scandinavian immigrants, the Germans maintained churches in which their native tongue was spoken at first; but they quickly yielded to English-speaking services, especially where the children attended the public school. Both groups have remained substantially rural in their vocational life, though the Mennonites fostered a larger measure of clannishness based upon the tenet of their faith that requires resistance to war. As one of the so-called "peace churches," the Mennonites have had a rallying point of greater specificity than some other denominations. Originally certain distinctions of dress served to differentiate them, but these have long since disappeared. It should be added, however, that though the Mennonites of Corn County belong to two different wings of the followers of Menno Simons they seem to be moving closer together in the present period. Worship and intensive Bible study have served as a reminder of their roots. Though few in number, they have made an impact disproportionate to the size of their total group.

Into this coagulation created by a mixture of British-American Yankees, Irish, Germans and Scandinavians has come one other sizable migrating group. It is composed of persons whose ancestors are also British-American in origin, having come originally from Scotland and the North of Ireland. Many generations of residence in Kentucky and Tennessee witnessed the departure from adherence to a strict Calvinism, and a loss of educational enthusiasm. Biblical dependence, often based on a literal interpretation of the Scriptures, came to characterize their religious activity. The region of their residence in America has acquired the designation "Bible Belt," though no specific lines of demarcation for this area could possibly be given to any single part of the nation. Both the southern highlands and the lowlands produced a larger crop of children than some other areas. Some of their descendants, such as Daniel Boone, went west to the Mississippi. Still others moved north of the Ohio River into southern Indiana and Illinois.

The family of Abraham Lincoln reflected the early stages of this movement. By the time of the First World War, with a labor shortage on the farms of the corn belt, many of these erstwhile Kentuckians came to settle in Corn County. One town, in fact, is occasionally referred to slyly as "Little Hodgenville," after the birthplace of Lincoln.

Since they came out of what was largely a frontier Baptist and Methodist background, it is scarcely to be wondered at that the newcomers did not find the more modestly emotional life of the churches previously established congenial to their type of religious expression. The type of Baptist church that the New England migrants established reflected the cultural and theological emphasis of Brown University, Newton Seminary and, later, Colgate Rochester Seminary and the University of Chicago. It seemed to lack something which the new migration from the South sought in Baptist churches. It required less than half a century for Baptist churches of the New England type to reflect an emphasis generally associated with Southern Baptist churches.

The Methodists, with their extraordinary capacity for meeting the conditions of the frontier and their vigorous promotion of ecclesiastical structures, had established units of their church in most of the evolving communities. The transplanted southerners from border states found their church there. The strong connectional system of the Methodists, their emphasis on a more unified educational program, and the reunion of the Methodist Churches North and South enabled them to maintain a continuity and thus resist the forces making for denominational selection.

Anyone even slightly familiar with religious life and institutions in America knows that the denominations referred to thus far do not constitute the full spectrum of church institutional life. On that spectrum and indeed representing a considerable band of it must be included numerous shadings of religious preference representing groups commonly lumped together as "Pentecostal." When one of the large Lutheran churches built a beautiful new sanctuary on the edge of Main Town, it was a Pentecostal congregation that bought the property previously occupied by the Lutherans.

Main Town has a Kingdom Hall, with a small but customarily aggressive company of Jehovah's Witnesses. Also in both Main Town and River Town there is a very small cluster of Jewish families congenially related to the life of the community.

From time to time other sects have come and gone. A catalog of them would read like a listing of the religious organizations of much of America. Here, however, are most of the major denominations commonly found in the Midwest.

More than a century of time has elapsed since the prairie was broken and the settlers founded the institutions that provided ties of continuity with their past. But they have lived in what is designated as an open society where there has been freedom to cross denominational, class, and political lines. The freedom was available and it was used, as the report of the study will describe. As the consequences of this intermingling unfold, some conclusions can be drawn about the influence of religion upon the people of this typical county and about the kind of religion that has been fostered here.

CHAPTER III

METHOD

AFTER IT WAS concluded that Corn County was typical of its region, it became necessary to devise a method that would give accurate portrayal of the information sought. (A volume providing a comprehensive portrayal of the methodology is available for those who desire further descriptions of the study.) The interview method was used and the data was secured over a period of approximately four years, two years being required for each phase of the interviewing. In the first period the purpose was to secure general information concerning the churches attended, frequency of attendance, participation in church organizational activities, and membership in voluntary associations outside the church organization. This portion of the study provided necessary data concerning educational attainment and economic position. The latter was secured by a rating of the type of house the interviewee occupied. The use of house type has been substantially established as a reliable index of economic position.

It was also possible to learn the type of work done by the interviewees. On the basis of this information it was possible to classify the respondents according to a standard classification using the two categories "white collar" and "blue collar."

Increasing attention has been paid in recent years to the question of social class. Whatever may be the presuppositions of religious groups based upon egalitarian principles of their faith, it would seem that all denominations have been affected by the same influences that make for class divisions in the rest of society. Education, economic level, and type of occupation have consciously or unconsciously served as selective factors in making up individual congregations and, to some degree at least, entire denominations.

There is a general assumption that educational and economic levels are correlated with intelligence. For purposes of this study, this correlation was not assumed until the second part of the study was conducted and the Thematic Apperception Test used to discern the general intelligence levels of adherents to various denominations.

LOCALITIES STUDIED

Five towns were selected originally for analysis. In addition to Main Town (the county seat town) and River Town, both described earlier, there was included Coal Village, a town of approximately one thousand population serving a prosperous agricultural area but also containing several small industries and a substantial coal strip mining project nearby. Serviceville is, likewise, a community of approximately one thousand and exists almost wholly as a farm service community. Elm Center is a hamlet with two hundred population, one store, and a church. In addition to the towns described, three rural farm townships were included. Elm Center, Coal Village, and one of the rural townships were studied only in the first phase of the total program.

The second phase of the study occupying the latter two years was primarily concerned with the ideas and attitudes of the individuals originally selected on a basis of random sampling. It became apparent that it was unnecessary to include all the communities that had originally been included in the first part of the study. Therefore, for the attitudinal, and actually the most important, portion of the study, it was decided to confine the interviewing to Main Town, River Town, Serviceville, and two open country townships. This still provided approximately twelve hundred interviews and substantially more than would have been necessary to get accurate results.

INSTRUMENTS

No attempt was made to construct an interview schedule that could be standardized as a test. The intent, instead, was to use questions relative to fairly common themes in religious thought and encourage the interviewee to elaborate freely. Categories of response were created by the researcher analysts.

So far as is known, no attempt has been made heretofore to utilize the Thematic Apperception Test for purposes of a study such as this. The procedure is described briefly in Chapter IX, "Denominational Influence on Psychological Characteristics."

It would have been better, of course, if the study could have been completed in a shorter period of time. The four-year span was not essential to the thoroughness of results. Funds to employ an adequate interviewing staff did not become available until the latter period of the study.

SAMPLING PROCESS

In Main Town a 25 per cent sample was taken of most church groups, and every fourth dwelling unit was used in the original sample. In Serviceville every second dwelling unit was selected, and in the open country every third unit was selected. It became apparent that because of the unique situation in River Town with its 60 per cent Catholic population dispersed among four churches, and with one Protestant church (Congregational), it was unnecessary to utilize so large a sample. The interviewing in the first phase of the study had established the approximate membership distribution by denomination.

In Serviceville every second nonchurch member was interviewed. In the open country the attempt was made to interview every adult in the dwelling unit selected.

As can well be surmised, not everyone co-operated with the interviewing. Every person, however, who came within the sample but refused to co-operate was approached at least three times, and the nature of the study was thoroughly explained. There were a number of instances in which families, because of either odd work hours or consistent absence from their residence, had to be called on as many as a dozen times in order for the full requirements of interviewing to be met and for the thoroughness of the study to be maintained.

Of the towns studied, Main Town has the largest number of churches, with fourteen. Included are the Roman Catholic church and the following active Protestant churches: Baptist, Christian, Congregational, Christian Science, Jehovah's Witnesses, Augustana Lutheran, United Lutheran, Methodist, Presbyterian, United Pentecostal, and Wesleyan

Methodist. The German Lutheran church is nearly defunct, and efforts were being made to organize an Episcopal church at the time this study was made.

In Serviceville there are six churches, including the Roman Catholic church and the following Protestant churches: Baptist, Episcopal, Methodist, Mennonite, and Pentecostal.

River Town has four Roman Catholic churches, one very small Greek Orthodox church, one practically defunct Jewish synagogue, and one Protestant church which is Congregational. The four Catholic churches are all ethnic churches, and local people would often refer to them by the name of the ethnic group dominant in each case—Irish, Italian, Polish, and Lithuanian. Of the four, the Irish church has the greatest proportion of people of mixed ethnic backgrounds.

There are two churches in the open country area, a Mennonite and a Congregational.

Anyone familiar with the Midwest will quickly detect the absence in this study of certain denominations that have strong membership representation in this region. In Corn County, for example, there are four Evangelical United Brethren churches. There are none, however, in the communities studied. In Serviceville there is a small Episcopal church with a part-time priest and when this study was being conducted, as indicated earlier, attempt was being made to establish a church of this denomination in Main Town. Likewise, there are a number of Bible churches and Pentecostal groups scattered throughout the county. In none of the communities studied did their membership constitute a sufficient group to provide a reliable sample.

Interviewing was conducted by staff and graduate students of the Federated Theological Faculty of the University of Chicago; some of the students and all of the staff were associated with the project from its start to its completion.

The responses were coded, punched on IBM cards, and machine-tabulated.

CHAPTER IV

CHURCH PARTICIPATION

ACTIVE PARTICIPATION in the life of an organization is, presumably, the principal index of interest. Church attendance becomes an important criterion of interest and response toward the church. Denominational yearbooks have a column for it and both ministers and church treasurers are highly sensitive to this column. Likewise, church members are consciously or unconsciously rated by their pastors on some kind of scale of attendance regularity. Cartoonists and ecclesiastical humorists find grist for their mills in the various reasons for absence from services of public worship.

Obviously the factors making for church attendance are many and complex. Table 1 indicates the frequency of church attendance by the people of Corn County. Behind these figures, however, are reasons that do not lend themselves to easy analysis. To what extent are they the result of the content of the worship service, the liturgy, the sociability of other attendants, the personality of the pastor, priest, or rabbi, family training, and innumerable other factors?

Worship and liturgy take on especial relevance at the present time because all the major denominations of America have been indicating increased interest in them. Theological seminaries reveal that both students and faculty are participating actively in this trend. The reasons explaining it are numerous and escape oversimplification. It is safe to presume that an interest in worship and what emerges from it constitutes a principal emphasis of religious institutions. Hence a closer look at what is experienced for worship is essential.

TABLE 1. *Frequency of Church Attendance Per Year in Per Cent for Protestants and Catholics by Type of Population Center*

	Less than 12 Times		12–40 Times		41 Times and Over		Total		N=	
Area	P.	C.	P.	C.	P.	C.	P.	C.	P.	C.
Main Town	33.7	13.6	27.7	9.9	38.6	76.5	100	100	668	81
River Town	38.7	17.1	34.3	15.1	27.0	67.8	100	100	137	445
Coal Village*	36.0	8.9	44.0	7.1	20.0	84.0	100	100	150	112
Serviceville	33.7	13.2	25.9	5.3	40.4	81.5	100	100	166	38
Elm Center*	16.4	14.3	23.0	0.0	60.6	85.7	100	100	61	14
Rural farm population of 3 townships	34.8	17.6	33.7	5.9	31.5	76.5	100	100	359	51

* Community used in early part of study but later omitted as unnecessary for providing adequate sample.

If "man's chief end is to glorify God" and to yield his total life to God's direction, then the manner in which this occurs takes on primary importance. Among an increasing number of church members, emphasis upon psychological betterment and focus on the narrower concept of the self seems to have had its day. The shaking of our security as a result of world forces has jarred men loose from an assumption that their own petty selves are God's chief concern. Perhaps with a bit of exaggeration it can be suggested that the theme song of the earlier period was the gospel hymn whose chorus contains the refrain, "Oh, that will be glory for *me*."

Each of the twelve hundred interviewees was asked the question, "When you attend church what are the main reasons that prompt you to go?" Most of the persons interviewed had given little thought to such a query; hence there was a certain amount of fumbling for an answer. Frequently the reply on first thought would be, "Why, you just go, I guess." Then, on a little further reflection, more cogent reasons emerged. A little patience on the part of the interviewer could facilitate the more substantial response.

The replies are divided roughly into two categories: (1) those which involve some emotional response based on a measure of meaning within the worship service itself and (2) those which indicated merely an expression of habit or the fulfillment of some social desire. Obviously, none of these is strictly pure and unadulterated in form. It would be impossible, for example, to separate genuine devotion from the overtones of friendship or the glow of good feeling and inner comfortableness that may come to a person whose friends are also present in the church. Similarly, an individual whose family roots are in a particular church and for whom the standards maintained by the family are identified with participation in that church might well continue in attendance out of custom and habit engendered by the family tradition.

In so far as some kind of division can be constructed, it would seem that there are recognizable reasons and a rough classification of the responses is possible. The first broad category can be designated as "internal." It includes in range what is historically deemed as traditional and basic to participation in the service of worship, that is, "to worship the Lord," as many expressed it. Under this same category would be included the psychological benefit that so many find in church attendance. Their response might well be, "I feel better for going." This could mean many things, but presumably it connotes what has historically been a result of participation in worship—a realization of forgiveness and a fresh beginning which follows an act of dedication and repentance.

The second broad category is designated as "external." It includes the replies of those persons who have based their church participation on habit and tradition. "I have just always gone," or "It's the thing to do."

Table 2 indicates the reasons for church attendance in the largest community in the study. These responses do not vary greatly from those of the other communities.

Perhaps a reverse way of discovering the meaning of church worship is to ask the reasons for nonparticipation. Here, however, the responses were standard and uniform, so that no real clue was offered. For the most part the factors impeding church attendance were the familiar ones of illness, travel, "company came," etc. As might be expected in a highly mobile society, travel constitutes a substantial bloc of the total reasons.

It will be noted from Table 2 that there are no startling variations on the part of the church members. The range of objective reasons is from 35 per cent and 36 per cent, for the Christian (Disciples) and Augustana Lutheran, to 61 per cent for the Mission Covenant. Among the Methodists, where the fellowship factor has been traditionally important, it is actually low in relation to the internal reasons.

It could be assumed that the so-called liturgical tradition

TABLE 2. *Reasons for Church Attendance in Per Cent for Selected Denominations—Main Town*

Church Membership of Respondent	N=	Reasons Cited					
		Internal				*External*	
		Objective	Mixed	Subjective	Tradition	Fellowship	All Others and "Don't know"
Baptist	44	55	14	25	23	25	7
Catholic	52	52	8	35	29	8	6
Christian	20	35	5	40	40	5	20
Congregational	73	47	12	43	26	16	7
Lutheran, Augustana	42	36	14	36	46	12	10
Lutheran, United	81	46	20	33	21	9	7
Methodist	82	46	11	42	18	17	4
Mission Covenant	54	61	9	28	37	20	6
Presbyterian	44	46	3	32	36	16	14
None	111	27	10	20	13	14	16

is more influential in disposing its adherents toward worship in its purer sense, leading them into an expression of devotion to their church based on a greater interest in worship. Such seems not to be the case. The findings indicate that no particular form of worship is productive of more devout church adherence or theological understanding than some other form.

From the data, one may hypothesize that forms of worship serve some other function than the development of devout participants, even though that might be the avowed purpose.

Forms of worship are identified with particular denominations, and participation in the life of a particular denomination may serve ends other than those traditionally regarded as spiritual. Too, they may be identified in the mind of the worshiper with fulfillment of a practice that is regarded as "church participation," the meaning of which may not be clear, but in his mind it is associated with the practices of religion. In so far as can be discerned from the study, there is little difference in the reasons given by members of various churches for participation in the services of worship. It can also be said that though the capacity to articulate the reasons for church attendance may be greater among persons who have a higher intellectual ability, here again there are not marked differences between the several churches.

What all this apparently means is that there are factors other than worship and liturgy which are conditioning the response of the members of the several churches.

Among the reasons for nonattendance, an interesting variation appears. Among the Baptists, Mission Covenant members, and Augustana Lutherans the proportion of those who gave external reasons for nonattendance was far greater than in the other denominations. These three churches have strongly differing forms of worship. Two of them reflect in their composition what was an ethnic emphasis. Therefore, their adherence to church attendance, as seen in the reasons given for absence, would indicate that not only is it the uniqueness or hold that the form of worship has upon them but rather is it that congenial association disposes them strongly toward attendance at worship.

In the response of men and women to church participation there is a substantially lower degree of interest on the part of men regardless of social class or intellectual ability. This ratio of difference is found in both Catholic and Protestant affiliation. The white-collar group is more critical of the church than the blue-collar group even though the numbers engaging in this criticism are very small. With this absence of any vigorous criticism on the part of the blue-collar group it could be inferred that nothing the church would do to comply with protests (since there were almost none) would make much difference in the appeal of the church to the blue-collar group. This is not to imply that reaching this group is impossible. It merely suggests that the present church procedures beget neither hostility nor acceptance.

Church loyalty is unconsciously identified with church attendance. One assumption behind this is the influence that supposedly can be exerted upon the attendant as a result of his physical presence at a service of worship. This in itself contains a presupposition about the nature of the church and its consequences to those associating closely with it. All of this is apparently implied in church attendance.

Reasons for church attendance may involve much more than what is associated with occupying a pew and participating in the liturgy, however simple. Recognizing fully that it is not possible to get clearly thought out and accurate descriptions of whatever it is that disposes individuals toward their church, it was thought that a free-flowing comment undirected by the interviewer would enable the interviewee to hint at some of the other reasons for church participation.

When the answers were classified they could be divided roughly into the categories of Table 3:

1. Worship and/or program
2. Quality of present minister or priest
3. Character of some church members
4. No outstanding elements

5. Everything liked
6. Other
7. "Don't know"

Originally it was contemplated that a separate category would be needed for "doctrine or belief." Presumably, a range from Roman Catholic to Baptist would bring forth some assertion of doctrinal difference or a basis of preference stemming from particular beliefs. This proved not to be the case. Allowance should be made, however, for varying ways of expressing this differentiation. It is possible that the expression of preference for a particular kind of worship program might be another means of identifying with doc-

TABLE 3. *Things Liked Most About Own Church in Per Cent for Selected Denominations—Main Town*

CHURCH MEMBERSHIP OF RESPONDENT	N=	ELEMENTS CITED						
		Worship and/or Program	*Quality of Present Minister or Priest*	*Character of Some Church Members*	*No Outstanding Elements*	*Everything Liked*	*Other*	*"Don't know"*
Baptist	42	40	10	55	7	0	36	5
Catholic	52	58	13	8	2	15	38	8
Christian	20	25	20	65	5	5	20	5
Congregational	73	62	11	26	3	0	23	14
Lutheran, Augustana	42	79	12	2	5	7	17	2
Lutheran, United	81	57	23	31	5	2	19	7
Methodist	82	52	28	29	7	1	17	6
Mission Covenant	54	63	15	28	2	7	13	4
Presbyterian	44	45	36	39	9	0	32	2
None	111	29	13	21	8	2	11	32

trine or belief. The fact that a high percentage of the persons above average in intellectual ability did specify that the worship service of their particular denomination appealed largely to them (67 per cent) may indicate this desire to include doctrine as a basis for predisposing the individual toward his church. Correspondingly, 43 per cent of the persons below average in intellectual ability indicated worship as that which drew them to their denomination.

RELIGIOUS LEADERSHIP

Traditionally, among Protestants at least, the personality and attractiveness of the minister have been influential factors in denominational selection. Interest in these qualities of the minister will be discussed later (Chapter VIII).

A somewhat puzzling disclosure in the data is the fact that the churches with congregational polity—Baptist, Congregational, Lutheran, and Mission Covenant—seem to be those in which the attraction of the minister is least influential, whereas the Methodist and Presbyterian churches rate this quality highest, 28 per cent and 36 per cent respectively. (The Christian [Disciples] denomination is not cited here because the number in the sample was so small.) It is, of course, possible that particular leaders at a given time in the history of these respective churches may markedly color the response, whereas under other leadership these figures might be substantially different. It should be noted, too, that the response of the Catholics to their priests is in the lower ranges.

The low percentage of Catholics who are drawn to their church for reasons of attraction toward the character of other church members is understandably small. No great significance should be attached to the figures for the Roman

Catholics or the Augustana Lutherans in this area. The size of the sample does not warrant having the conclusions commensurate with the apparently low response. As a matter of general interest it can again be pointed out how similar the response of the United Lutherans is to that of the Presbyterians, Methodists, and Congregationalists.

In response to "worship," the Catholics in River Town indicate less enthusiasm than their fellow Catholics in Main Town and the open country. On the other hand, River Town is much more interested in the quality of its priests and the character of its fellow members as sources of attraction to their church. As was indicated, this latter factor is insignificant in Main Town, Serviceville, or the open country. One conclusion to be drawn from this is that where Catholics are in a minority, they are more conscious of the distinctiveness of their forms of worship and of uniqueness in their faith which distinguishes them from those around them.

For both Catholics and Protestants in the four areas, any dislike for the professional religious leadership is very small.

In those churches in which life of the institution centers around social activities in a larger measure and in which class distinction determines the extent of personal relationships, it is to be understood why stronger feelings relative to personalities may generate. In Main Town, Serviceville, and the open country, approximately one fourth of the Protestants indicate that their dislike focuses on the character of other church members. In Serviceville, for example, the figure is 29 per cent for Protestants, as against 0.0 for Catholics. How much of this can be attributed to the fact that in Serviceville there is one Catholic church, while there are five Protestant churches in close proximity can only be estimated. The situation may be further accentuated by the fact that Serviceville is a static community, if not actually declining, having lost population over the past quarter century. It can only be hypothesized that where attention in the life of the church is focused upon a force or power outside the community, there is less likelihood of friction than where the life of the institution focuses more substantially on the relationships of people who comprise the organization.

Though attention has here been given to some of the qualities and aspects of the church that are least liked, it must be added that by far the largest percentage for most of the churches was in the column indicating "no negative elements." It can only be inferred, therefore, that there is general approval of the life of their church and a goodly measure of devotion to it. But it is the individual of above average intellectual ability who is likely to find negative elements. Correspondingly, the blue-collar worker is least likely to find fault with his church.

In the study of attitudes toward one's church a note appears that seems to be largely present in every other phase of the study, namely, the lack of any particular interest in theological foundations or the belief structures which might differentiate the several denominations.

Forms of worship often characterize denominations. Presumably, these are grounded in theological beliefs and are of some significance in the selection of a religious institution. It would appear that factors other than beliefs and theological convictions are determinative in denominational affiliation.

DENOMINATIONAL PREFERENCES AND INDIVIDUAL STATUS

One of the phenomena of American life is the ease with which people move across denominational lines. Differences that at one time seemed important because of nationality background or distinguishing characteristics of worship, the role of Biblical authority, or the status ascribed to the clergyman have been factors determining the choice of denominational affiliation. People dislocated by war industries, or transplanted by a new assignment from a corporation with production or distribution centers scattered across the nation, find themselves easily at home in a church affiliated with a denomination heretofore unknown to them. To countless thousands of people, a church was a church. Its denomination was of secondary importance.

An unpleasant subject related to denominations is that of status—unpleasant because its very presuppositions seem to deny the equality of man before God. The Christian apologist contends that the ground at the foot of the cross is level. There are no class or caste distinctions there. It has become embarrassing, therefore, to acknowledge that individual churches and sometimes whole denominations have become identified with a class position.* With the growing interest on the part of sociologists in studying the phenomenon of class structure in American life, churches as institutions of the community have come under the same observation, and similar criteria for appraising them have been used.

Possibly in no other way does Corn County reveal its typicality more than in the status structure of its churches. The mobility of its people in transferring from one denomination to another and the rise of the denominations with which later arrivals to the county become affiliated are a national phenomenon. Paralleling these changes is the relative de-

* See H. Richard Niebuhr's study, *The Social Sources of Denominationalism* (Henry Holt & Co., 1929); Warner and Others, *Democracy in Jonesville* (Harper & Brothers, 1949); Vidich and Bensman, *Small Town in Mass Society* (Princeton University Press, 1958); Goldschmidt, *As You Sow* (Harcourt Brace and Company, Inc., 1947).

cline of some of the older and previously stronger churches and denominations. As was indicated in Chapter II, the pioneers who first came to this prairie country brought with them their institutions. A strong interest in education, however, led their young people away from rural life and to the metropolitan centers. The successive waves of migration brought their own institutions. As members of these several migrating groups arrived later, they established themselves in occupations, in economic life, and in the ownership of property. Since these individuals operated within the openness of American society and its opportunity for economic advancement, it is to be understood why in a normal period of time they have either identified themselves with the institutions already present or have brought to positions of stability and prominence the institutions with which they had traditionally been related.

Basing their judgment upon numerous studies of communities and religious organizations, as well as on their own first-hand experience with church life in many other places as well as in Corn County, the persons responsible for the study hypothesized that factors other than creed and belief largely affect denominational affiliation. To test this hypothesis, therefore, the interviewees were asked the question, "Which church is most like your own and which is least like your own—and why?" That the Disciples and the Baptists each regarded the other as most like itself is understandable. Both practice immersion, they are congregational in polity and are composed of native American stock. It is also significant, however, that these two churches are so nearly alike in economic, educational, and intellectual levels. It is also understandable that the Congregationalists and the Presbyterians indicated overwhelmingly their conviction that the other was most like themselves. This too, presumably, can be explained in terms of the close parallel between them in economic, educational, and intellectual levels. It is perhaps further to be understood in the light of the fact that a century ago they were one church composed of the New England stock that first came into the county. Division occurred as a result of difference in opinion over the amount of emphasis to be accorded the slavery issue. Subsequently, each of these churches has become a rallying place for those seeking fewer restrictions on the part of their former denomination and, possibly, the opportunity for associating with those who were already in the leadership positions of the county.

The thriving Mission Covenant church of Swedish background indicated a preponderance of preference for, and felt itself most nearly like, the Augustana Lutherans, who, like themselves, possessed a Swedish background. Very few felt they resembled the Congregationalists (5 per cent) or the Presbyterians (7 per cent). A substantial number, however, sensed kinship with the Methodists (19 per cent) and the Baptists (12 per cent). The Methodists, on the other hand, indicated by far the largest measure of interest in the Congregationalists (29 per cent) and the Presbyterians (21 per cent). Numerically the Methodists are the strongest church in Main Town and their people hold positions of prestige and responsibility. Their leaders co-operate with and are related to the Congregational and Presbyterian leaders in all civic activities. Too, at a time when there was some unpleasantness in the Congregational fellowship, a number of leaders of that church transferred to the Methodist.

The United Lutheran and the Augustana Lutheran communicants expressed a similarity of creed and of form of worship. Each, interestingly, rates very low the characteristics of the other group as a factor in attraction, whereas both the Presbyterian and Congregational members indicate that it is the characteristics of the members of the other church which attract them more than similarity of creed.

An additional way of arriving at self-identification and interrelationship of denominations is to discover which church seems to be the least like one's own. As might be expected, Protestants overwhelmingly attested to the fact that the Catholic church was least like theirs; but then, which church other than the Catholic would seem least like their own? The response to this query, again not wholly unexpected, revealed the fact that the Pentecostal type church least resembled their own. Frequently in the replies reference was made to the amount of noise that characterized the Pentecostal service, inferring possibly a lack of dignity. This might also be related to the fact that the Pentecostal churches had the highest percentage of blue-collar constituents, and persons of average and below average intellectual ability.

The largest measure of unfamiliarity and lack of information concerning other denominations was among the Roman Catholics. It would appear that they had been substantially walled off from any consideration of the basic beliefs of Protestantism. On the other hand, aside from some fairly general ideas about the nature of Catholicism, Protestants could hardly be said to possess extensive information about the Roman Catholic Church either. One cannot but conclude that relations between the denominations are on an emotive basis rather than upon the foundation of any real understanding of what is deemed basic in the religious life of the adherent to another faith. In the same breath it must be commented that very few of the individuals interviewed had any profound understanding of the history and the basic beliefs of their own denominations. For the ecumenical movement the implications of this mutual lack of information would be hard to exaggerate. Where emotional, status, and other sociopsychological factors are determinative, the possibilities for real co-operation are not impressive.

FRIENDSHIP AND CHURCH MEMBERSHIP

As indicated earlier, many Protestants feel that the degree of friendliness prevailing in their church constitutes a factor in its attractiveness to them. Not many would be likely to spell this out in terms of a rationale for Protestantism, but certainly the emphasis upon friendliness is very important in the life of the church in Protestantism. If the church consists of persons who are called out of the world to form a fellowship which shall witness to God's way among men, the quality of human relationships becomes one index of the church's vitality. Congeniality and a mutual concern in making its witness would, it would seem, be reflected in the quality of friendly life exhibited among the members.

In a highly mobile society where individuals cross denominational lines as easily as is now the case, and where so high a premium is placed upon conformity with the totality of society, it is hardly likely that many church groups will feel called upon to exhibit a variation from the rest of society. Where members of a dozen or more congregations in a community work side by side with the members of other churches in performing their occupational tasks, and where they intermingle with others in their residences, and where they are brought together on common ground in dealing with school affairs, civic matters, and recreational activities, it would be difficult to maintain strong differences even if there were some justification for them on a basis of belief, which apparently there is not.

Unfortunately there are no data indicating the church affiliation of the closest friends of the church members of Corn County a generation or two ago. We can only rely on the oft-expressed testimony on the part of the interviewees that both they themselves and their parents were more likely to find their closest friends among the members of their own churches twenty-five years earlier.

The choice of one's friends, the type of work in which they are engaged, and the way in which the friendship originated throw some light upon the contemporary patterns of friendship formation and the degree to which the church affiliation is at present determinative. Roughly, about one fourth to one third of the friends of church members seem to come from the same church. Or, to express it another way, approximately two thirds to three fourths of the friends of church members of Corn County come from churches other than their own. Of great significance, too, is the fact that Catholic-Protestant friendships figure so prominently in the data, particularly in the town that is so predominantly Catholic, River Town. Here, among the members of the Congregational church, the only Protestant church in the town, 62 per cent of the persons named as closest friends were members of the Catholic church. Catholic members indicated that 15 per cent of their best friends were Protestants.

In dominantly Protestant Main Town, Catholics indicate that only 38 per cent of their closest friends are Catholics. Meanwhile, Protestants attest that 32 per cent of their closest friends are in their own church and 55 per cent in other denominations. The Catholic pattern seems to be paralleled also in Serviceville and in the open country where in each case Catholic friendships are 35 per cent but their Protestant friendships are 48 per cent and 60 per cent respectively. From this one infers that not only is there little alienation but, rather, a substantial measure of co-operativeness and sociability across Catholic-Protestant lines. This is true in all the areas, but the Protestant outreach toward Catholics is substantially greater than the reverse in River Town.

Even though there is so high a measure of Protestant-Catholic association, it has not led to thoughtful consideration of the respective tenets of each other's faith. Frequently it was commented, "We just don't talk about things like that." Obviously, religion is not something about which individuals can converse objectively or about which they know enough to share meaningful concepts. This would seem to substantiate what has been indicated previously and what is to follow, as it relates to the basic ideas of religious faith.

Are there denominations whose people still find their friendships primarily among fellow members? It may be significant that Baptists, Congregationalists, United Lutherans, Methodists, and Presbyterians are almost identical in the percentage of friends in their own denomination (Table 4). In each case their friends are predominantly in other denominations. Again, the exception to this pattern are the Augustana Lutherans and the Mission Covenant members (41 per cent and 60 per cent respectively). These churches, which still represent the largest percentage of representatives of Scandinavian background, maintain a friendship-exclusiveness pattern more nearly like that of a generation ago when a large number of first-generation and Swedish-born

TABLE 4. *Church Membership of Three Closest Friends in Per Cent for Selected Denominations—Main Town*

CHURCH MEMBERSHIP OF RESPONDENT	N=	CHURCH MEMBERSHIP OF THREE CLOSEST FRIENDS				
		Catholic	*Protestant*			*None*
			Same		Other	
Baptist	135	4	30		59	7
Catholic	156	38		52		10
Christian	60	7	25		57	11
Congregational	224	6	32		57	5
Lutheran, Augustana	126	3	41		51	5
Lutheran, United	237	8	33		55	4
Methodist	242	12	32		50	6
Mission Covenant	162	2	60		36	2
Presbyterian	132	7	29		59	5
None	321	15		72		13

members made up the rolls of those churches. It must be added, however, that there are signs of change. As of 1960, the Augustana Lutheran Church voted to merge with two other large Lutheran bodies, including the United Lutheran, which has been traditionally the most liberal of the Lutheran groups.

SOCIABILITY AND FRIENDSHIP

Fostering of sociability is one of the phenomena of American church life. American visitors to Europe are quite mindful of the absence of kitchens and fellowship rooms in European churches. Fellowship and group life, even to bowling alleys and handcraft departments, are a reflection of American interest in social life. Whether this is because of the influence of fraternal groups and service clubs or whether they are the answer to the same call that produced the large-scale socializing in American churches will never be accurately diagnosed. Suffice it to say they are a part of the American phenomenon.

Have the numerous group activities that characterize almost every American church—women's societies, youth groups, golden-age clubs, musical organizations, and many others—served to recruit members for the church or to provide fellowship for them after they became members? This is another chicken-and-the-egg question. It is incontestable, however, that friendships in large number have been generated through these activities. The YMCA and YWCA came into existence and have thrived partly because of a need not being met by the churches. Some of that need was the opportunity for friendship among individuals of a particular age group. Now one asks whether these organizations, especially those in churches, serve the function they were once intended to provide. It must be quickly added that many churches have intelligently made adaptations as the times changed. If the function of friendship groups—and to this must be added the total life of the church—has performed the service of relating people more consistently to the life of the church, it would probably be revealed in the extent of close friendship generated through the church relationship.

With the exception of Serviceville, the number of persons who met their closest friends through church activities is very small, and even there among Protestants, the highest group recorded, the number is only one fifth of the total number of friends. It is conclusive that forces other than the church are making for the close friendships of Corn County people.

For specific denominations in Main Town, only the Mission Covenant and Augustana Lutheran again exceed one fifth, and even in these instances the increase is not large (Augustana Lutheran, 24 per cent; Mission Covenant, 38 per cent).

Though again the differences are small, twice as many individuals of above-average intellectual ability find their friends through church activities as do the below-average group. It might be inferred from this that some of the more thoughtful people believe their friendships are reinforced and are even more desirable if made and sustained in relation to a church.

To the extent that these data are reliable, it would seem that one's church affiliation is not likely to be the largest determinative factor in the development of friendship. From this it cannot be deduced that the role of the church is not that of inspiring and encouraging friendship. It may well be that the very absence of specificity in church life and too much emphasis on generalities have reduced the possibilities of meaningful friendship. Perhaps one of the roles of the church of the future is to establish standards in its own life so high that superior qualities of friendship may be fostered.

CLASS AND CHURCH PARTICIPATION

It is a common assumption in America that there is uneven participation in church activities between white-collar and blue-collar workers. Church participation itself may constitute one of the factors serving to accentuate differences between white- and blue-collar workers. Protestant churches have not been singularly successful in attracting persons who are broadly categorized as "labor." Lest it seem primarily and solely an indictment of Protestantism, however, it must be noted that the Catholic Church is also gravely apprehensive about the loss of those who make up the ranks of labor.

The popular image of American life is that of middle-class individuals. Journals with the widest circulation foster that image. Correspondingly, the standard portrayal of the church attendant and the church structure itself seems to be that of the suburban member and his family, or perhaps for nostalgic reasons a country church is pictured. The Protestant participant in the service, however, is most frequently represented as the well-dressed suburbanite rather than as the farmer sitting in the pew in his shirt sleeves. In view of the population trend in the United States, this is a correct portrayal of what is typically American.

In Main Town, of the three categories of church attendance, the highest percentage among Protestants is that of the extremely faithful, who attend forty-one times a year or more. This is exceeded only by the participation in Serviceville and Elm Center. Each of these communities, it should be noted, has a high percentage of retired farmers and persons who, though they themselves are not actively engaged in farming, are in consultative or farm service relationships and have a farm background. The abnormally high participation registered in Elm Center may derive from the particular ministerial leadership at the time the study was made. The number of Catholics who attend service with greatest regularity is approximately twice or more the Protestant record. Despite this fact, Elm Center had the largest percentage of persons not active in any religious institution (29.9 per cent). The figure is almost as great for the rural farm townships (28.2 per cent). The fact that by far the largest percentage of the unchurched residents of the hamlet, Elm Center, fall within the blue-collar classification may serve to give some indication as to the basis for nonparticipation even though the community as a whole has the best record of loyalty to their church as indicated by frequency of attendance.

With the exception of River Town, the ratio of white-collar to blue-collar numbers for Protestant and Catholic is very nearly alike. The difference in River Town is, obviously, to be explained by the fact that, as a town populated heavily with industrial workers and approximately two thirds Catholic in composition, the percentage of white-collar workers in the Catholic churches is low (16.7 per cent vs. 83.3 per cent).

Coal Village and Serviceville are approximately equal in size, though Coal Village has about three times as many Catholics as Serviceville, due to the presence of Belgian coal miners who had been identified with that industry since it began operation. In Serviceville, participation in extra church activities is substantially greater than is the case in Coal Village. In predominantly Protestant Serviceville, with its six churches, there apparently have been sponsored more church-night suppers, men's clubs, women's organizations, and special denominational activities than is the case in the fewer churches of Coal Village.

The combination of facts—(1) the larger percentage of Protestant church membership in Serviceville and (2) the higher percentage of activity in extra church events—would seem to indicate that the six churches make provision for fuller participation on the part of Serviceville people than do the smaller number of Coal Village churches. Some doubt about this is cast by the fact that the percentage of nonchurch members is almost the same in the two communities (26.8 per cent for Coal Village and 28 per cent for Serviceville). It may be concluded that the larger number of churches has made possible a fuller engagement in church life than in the community with half as many churches.

When the rural farm population is added to the Serviceville population, the six churches would have an average base of five hundred. If an area similar to the open country townships around Serviceville is added to Coal Village, there would be a population base of approximately three thousand people for the three churches, or an average of one thousand per church. Thus, whatever else may be responsible for the participation disparity characterizing the churches, it is apparent that there is a higher measure of participation relationship in the community where the ratio of people to church is lower. Can it be hypothesized that individuals seek more opportunity for social expression and desire fellowship in more limited groups, and therefore the lower ratio is to be encouraged? This would seem to be a dubious hypothesis as against such factors as the more adequate church program, better educational opportunities, more substantial equipment, better music, and possibly better ministerial leadership where the population base is larger. Neither is the hypothesis aided by the Coal Village situation. Its two Protestant churches are small, and in order to sustain a resident ministry their ministers serve churches in other communities also. On the other hand, in Serviceville three of the churches maintain full-time resident ministers.

A question involving both economics and effectiveness is in order here: for the amount of money required of each member of the five Protestant churches of Serviceville or the two Protestant churches of Coal Village to finance their institutions, could not a more inclusive and profitable program of church life be secured? It is commonly understood that the per capita costs of the small church exceed those classed as "large." Anyone looking objectively at these communities cannot refrain from speculating on the possibilities if corresponding amounts were spent in a collective venture in co-operative church life.

The white-collar portion of each of the communities is more highly represented in the churches than it is in the community at large. Whereas, for example, they represent only 49.6 per cent of the population of Main Town, they are represented in the Protestant churches at a level of 56.6 per cent and in the Catholic church 61.1 per cent. A similar edge in favor of the white-collar contingent prevails in each of the other communities, with the exception of River Town, where the per cent of white-collar participants is almost twice its population per cent in the total community. This presumably can be explained in part on the grounds of the minority status which the Protestant population experiences in River Town; i.e., in its minority position it has stressed appeal to other white-collar residents and has thus become class selective.

While the white-collar contingent is overrepresented among the Protestants, the blue-collar group is underrepresented in the churches of each of the communities; i.e., the percentage of blue-collar individuals in the total population is higher than that in any of the total Protestant membership in each of the towns. On the other hand, with the exception of Main Town Catholics, where they are underrepresented as against the total population, in each of the other towns the blue-collar Catholics are almost exactly proportionate to the total representation of the community.

Thus, though there are single churches in the communities studied which may have a more equal representation of blue-collar constituents, for the most part it must be concluded that the Protestant churches in their membership have a less proportionate percentage of blue-collar constituents. The suggestion that there is a class bias attached to the Protestant churches seems to be substantiated. With a fifth of each community unchurched, and the largest percentage of those being blue-collar, there seems to be a field for "outreach."

CHAPTER V

BIBLICAL UNDERSTANDING

For most people of Corn County, their Sunday school curriculums have been built largely around Biblical materials, and the adult Bible classes have been what their name implies. In addition, much of the preaching has been Biblically related, even if not actually designed to correlate Biblical imagery with the contemporary scene. It might be hypothesized, therefore, that church people with so substantial a background of Biblical emphasis would be reasonably well informed about major ideas, personalities, and the implications of the Bible for the life of people today. As was true of some previously expressed hypotheses, the findings do not support this one either.

The churches with the higher educational and economic level indicated that they did not desire a Biblical fundamentalist for their leader, but there is little indication that any more comprehensive or enlightened interpretations of the Scriptures are substituted for the rejected fundamentalism. A low level of comprehension of Biblical meanings characterizes all denominations of Corn County regardless of education or degree of Biblical study.

In the preliminary testing period, questions were included that asked for information about specific Old Testament prophets and about several of the better-known parables of Jesus. It became apparent that so extensive a set of questions was unnecessary. The level of the questions was therefore reduced to that of seeking to discern any understanding of difference between Old and New Testament, or of anything the Hebrew prophets symbolized or stressed. It was decided to limit inquiry about the teaching of Jesus to a single parable—that of the good Samaritan.

OLD AND NEW TESTAMENT DIFFERENCES

Responses to a question about the difference between the Old and the New Testament covered a broad spectrum ranging from chronology ("The Old Testament is older than the New") to a distinction between law and love, or the New Testament as the instrument of salvation. Included also was the suggestion that the Old Testament predicts the life of Jesus and the New Testament tells about it.

Biblical content and the importance of the several divisions of the Bible seem not to constitute an important part of the religious education of Catholics. For that reason it may not be wholly fair to compare them in Biblical understanding with Protestants who, theoretically at least, have given a substantial amount of time at the adult level to Bible classes, listening to Scripture-reading, and to preaching which was Biblically related.

Main Town Catholics possessed the highest percentage of general understanding of Catholics in all of the communities studied; but even there, more than two thirds were unaware of any difference between the two principal divisions of the Bible. In River Town the percentage of the uninformed reached 92 per cent. In Serviceville it was 87 per cent, and in the open country about the same, 86 per cent.

Among the Protestants of Main Town, approximately three fifths could designate a difference between the Old and New Testament. In River Town, it may be that the Protestant pattern of Biblical familiarity is determined by the same factors that influence the Catholic majority. Either the leadership has not been effective in increasing Biblical comprehension or resistance resulting from a combination of conditions has made it impossible—or both. At any rate, 63 per cent of the Protestants indicate no knowledge of any difference.

Response by denomination in Main Town may illumine further the type and degree of comprehension by the several denominations (Table 5). The Methodists ranked highest in subjective response but were lowest in theological comprehension. Added to that, they presented almost the highest percentage of those who were unaware of any difference between the Old and the New Testament—"almost," because they were slightly surpassed in that dubious distinction by the United Lutherans (51 per cent) and the Congregationalists (48 per cent). The Methodists and Congregationalists have historically been regarded as concerned with the "religious growth" of their people and as placing stress upon their educational programs rather than upon liturgies and public worship.

The Mission Covenant church, with the lowest percentage of "Don't know" replies, had, as might be expected, the highest percentage response in the theological interpretation of the respective emphases of the two Biblical divisions. It would appear that intensive Biblical interpretation and study had been going on in this denomination. The correlation between the pronounced familiarity and a tendency

TABLE 5. *Differences Between the Old Testament and the New Testament in Per Cent for Selected Denominations—Main Town*

CHURCH MEMBERSHIP OF RESPONDENT	N=	DIFFERENCES CITED						
		Subjective—N. T. Easier to Comprehend	*Prophecy-Fulfillment Couplet*	*Law-Love Couplet*	*Salvation in N. T.*	*Historical*	*Other*	*"Don't know"*
Baptist	44	27	16	14	25	30	16	25
Catholic	52	14	6	12	12	12	10	68
Christian	20	15	10	5	40	20	15	30
Congregational	71	17	6	4	18	13	14	48
Lutheran, Augustana	42	31	21	14	17	14	12	36
Lutheran, United	81	22	10	7	15	9	9	51
Methodist	82	35	4	10	7	6	11	45
Mission Covenant	54	19	44	35	43	24	9	11
Presbyterian	44	18	25	14	23	21	27	27
None	63	11	8	2	8	6	11	67

toward social conservatism, as revealed later, raises some interesting questions. In addition, it was frequently true that when the interviewer would ask for further explication of the meaning of the replies there was noticeable absence of definition. This led to the conclusion that some of the definitions had been arrived at in catechetical or memorization fashion.

THE OLD TESTAMENT PROPHETS

With so small a percentage of church members possessing an understanding of the Old and New Testament difference, it would be unlikely that any response much different could be expected on a question of the meaning of the Old Testament prophets. The results, therefore, were not unexpected. Omitting the Catholic responses, which would be understandably high in the "Don't know" column, the replies from the other denominations do not differ greatly. In Main Town, 64 per cent could tell nothing about the Hebrew prophets; in River Town, 81 per cent; Serviceville, 62 per cent; and in the open country, surprisingly, only 41 per cent. The explanation for the latter would possibly derive from the inclusion of a cluster of Mennonite families living in the open country townships studied. In the Main Town division of churches there are too few Mennonites to be included in the sample, so that this does not constitute one of the major denominations cited. However, in the open country area where they colonized seventy-five years ago, they have maintained a vigorous denominational life.

There is so much that is colorful and charged with intense human interest in the Old Testament that where people have heard the stories narrated from pulpit or in adult classes, one would expect some lasting retention of their content.

Jeremiah with the yoke about his shoulders and Hosea with his unfaithful but accepted wife, Isaiah pleading with a people in captivity and Amos thundering against the nations, present vivid images of dynamic characters in Hebrew history. Is our unfamiliarity with the message and purpose of these prophets due to our being in a generation that disavows or is uncomfortable in the presence of judgment? Or are we so caught up in the fast-moving times that there is insufficient room in our schedules for a consideration of individuals who analyzed the meaning of their own times with great accuracy? Undoubtedly there are many reasons to explain the predominance of disinterest in the message of the Hebrew prophets either for their times or for our own.

A higher educational level is no guarantee that members of particular churches will have fuller comprehension of Biblical meanings. More than half the Presbyterian and Congregational members had no knowledge of the Old Testament prophets. In their uninformedness they are exceeded slightly by the Methodists, United Lutherans, Augustana Lutherans, and Disciples (Table 6).

For persons who could respond, the principal replies are in the areas of prophecy and theological interpretation. In neither of these divisions nor, with exception of the Mission Covenant, with both together, do as many as 50 per cent of the respondents have an explanation. The Presbyterians have a slight edge in the theological interpretation. And for

TABLE 6. *Meaning of the Old Testament Prophets in Per Cent for Selected Denominations—Main Town*

CHURCH MEMBERSHIP OF RESPONDENT	N=	MEANING CITED			
		Prophecy	*Theological and/or Moral*	*Other*	*"Don't know"*
Baptist	43	12	30	12	56
Catholic	52	10	14	2	77
Christian	19	5	11	16	74
Congregational	69	12	22	7	65
Lutheran, Augustana	42	26	10	5	62
Lutheran, United	80	10	15	6	74
Methodist	81	6	17	6	74
Mission Covenant	54	43	33	0	33
Presbyterian	44	16	36	14	60
None	67	5	8	3	87

reasons that might make for interesting analysis, men possess a somewhat better grasp of the theological and moral meaning than do women. Whether this is because the Hebrew prophets we know best are men or whether the issues they dealt with have generally been of more interest to men cannot be stated positively. Perhaps it is because men have been more inclined to deal with political matters. This is, at best, a conjecture.

THE PARABLE OF THE GOOD SAMARITAN

If church members did not know about the good Samaritan or the prodigal son, the chances are they would be uninformed about other parables as well. As is true of all the parables of Jesus, the parable of the good Samaritan contains meanings that hold the attention of individuals of all ages and intelligence levels. Therefore, the kinds of response given to the inquiry reflect the full spectrum from the simplest to the most profound. But the limited comprehension of the meaning of this story on the part of adults apparently results from concentrating primarily upon the moving nature of the drama rather than upon the profound meaning contained in it.

The high percentage of Protestants who conceived the meaning of this story as involving help to those in distress is gratifying. But is there not some significance in the fact that of the twelve hundred interviewed, no one expressed the idea that the way the Samaritan gave of himself to the injured man paralleled God's outpouring of himself to man with no expectation of return? Correspondingly, man may give of himself to his fellow man.

Perhaps it is unfair even to suggest that such an interpretation be made. This interpretation implies a theological reasoning and familiarity that has not been characteristic of preaching or Bible study in recent times. The current emphasis on Biblical theology does not find a parallel in immediately preceding generations. Hence there is little disposition to use theological thought structures for relating Biblical materials to contemporary life. It will be interesting to see whether the heightened interest in Biblical theology now so apparent in theological seminaries will find response among church people now unaware of any relationship between Biblical narratives and their symbolism and the contemporary human scene.

To discover that less than one third of their people find in the good Samaritan parable an admonition to provide aid to others, or, to express it another way, to learn that more than a third of their people had no idea of any meaning that might be attached to this parable would probably be a source of consternation to the Methodists, the United Lutherans, and the Congregationalists. The Presbyterians present a slightly better picture of response on the respective categories, indicating acquaintance with the meaning of the parable. This may be due in some measure to the fact, as was discovered during the course of the interviewing, that the pastor of the Presbyterian church had been preaching on the general theme of the good Samaritan and his congregation in Main Town were somewhat better informed and possessed more recent acquaintance with the parable than was true of some of the others. As one interviewee commented, "Thank goodness, Mr. B. has been preaching on this or we would have been in trouble."

The over-all response to the discussion of the parable raises certain fundamental questions. Why is it, for example, that some of the denominations with a disproportionate number of members possessing above-average intellectual ability are among the lowest in comprehension of the good Samaritan's meaning? It is true that persons with above-average intellectual ability are more capable of replying in conventional or satisfactory fashion to the question of the parable's meaning and correspondingly have fewer respondents in the "Don't know" column. Even so, the persons of above-average intellectual ability show a substantial lack of familiarity with the purpose of the parable, as is true of most of the other members of their churches. One cannot but conclude that there has been a deficiency of Biblical interpretation in almost all the denominations, and that some of the profounder meanings of Biblical insights have not been communicated. As this is true of persons of average and above-average intellectual ability, it is even more true of those who are in the below-average category, 60 per cent of whom are to be found in the "Don't know" column.

SOME CONSIDERATIONS

Dangerous though it may be to draw premature conclusions from the data at hand, one cannot but ponder the fact that so small a percentage of Protestants living in the open country appear in the "Don't know" column, and that they are the highest in percentage of persons who seem to recognize in the parable an injunction to aid others. Is it possible that in the rural areas there is still a greater capacity to understand a fundamental meaning of this parable than is the case for people who live in towns and small cities? One might draw such an inference from these data. The Bible is heavily weighted with rural ideology; its references are perhaps more readily grasped by rural people. It is understandable, therefore, why there is concern whether, after the migration from rural areas has ceased, an urban America can acquire and maintain the kind of understanding of the needs of others which Biblical narrative and ideology supports. At present the assumption seems to be popular that it is rural life which is carrying the value of mutual aid and concern. This, in the light of the religious education and church experience they had, is doubtful. It is at least worthy of note that the farm people in the study are pronouncedly superior in their understanding of the meaning of this parable.

In conclusion it must be commented that in Corn County —and, if it is truly representative, this is presumably true in other areas as well—the kind of understanding of the Biblical material and its relevance for the life of our own period is only slightly comprehended. Whether this result is the consequence of a generation or more of theological seminary graduates who themselves have not come to grips with the relevance of Biblical imagery for the common life can hardly be charged. May it be that the very circumstances in which the people of Corn County find themselves, their preoccupation with so many other interests and the seeming primacy that must be accorded these interests, makes irrelevant the type of insight and suggestion that might come from Biblical acquaintance? Perhaps a combination of both factors is responsible. Biblical imagery and insight may require a degree of skillfulness in interpretation that most communicators of the religious message are incapable of making. When their message is conveyed through the Biblical illustration, religious leaders are faced with the difficult task of translating the fundamental significance into relevant contemporary meaning.

Biblical authoritativeness has long since ceased to be effective for its own sake. That there is an authority in the Biblical record is scarcely deniable, but to use the Biblical record as a coercive device for the sake of impressing individuals with authority seems to have spent itself, despite the influence of some prominent evangelists.

One is led to ask whether an experiment might be attempted to provide a Biblical interpretation for persons of above-average intelligence as a means of making a beginning along this line. Already there are signs of initiation of such ventures, but they are for the most part in urban areas. There is nothing of this sort in Corn County at the time of this writing.

CHAPTER VI

THEOLOGICAL FOUNDATIONS

It is a function of theology to guide and to give definition to beliefs about God. Individuals whose lives are ordered by well-defined beliefs are likely to be more consistent and stable than those who are pushed around by gusts of doctrine or the whims and purposes of those persons who would use individuals for their own ends.

When we attest to the importance of God in our personal and collective life, this is a theological affirmation. Therefore it is important to know what theological foundations underlie the individual and corporate life of a community or nation.

Americans make much of the fact that they are a godly people, and Corn Countians are almost uniform in their insistence upon theistic devotion. But also, because this county, like most of the nonmetropolitan areas of the corn belt, is Christian in religious affiliation, it is assumed that "Christian standards" are dominant.

Since no survey of Christian beliefs and their implications for individual and social life was taken a century ago, there is no way of judging whether theological beliefs are more or less clearly defined now than was the case when the various migrating groups came to the Midwestern prairie. The presence of numerous churches and in most instances quite active religious education organizations within those churches would imply that members took seriously the tenets and beliefs officially espoused by both the local churches and the denominations of which they are a part.

Religious belief and personal devotion are not easily evaluated. Any attempt to comprehend the depth and seriousness of the belief structure of Corn Countians must necessarily be limited and incomplete. There are many queries and criteria for evaluating religious understanding. It seemed to the people conducting the study that there are certain major areas of belief that provide a clue to the kind of understanding that church people may have concerning the fundamentals of their faith. Three of these areas were explored in the present study:

1. *Distinctiveness of Christianity*

In a majority culture it is almost axiomatic that there is little pressure to justify the ideas and beliefs of the people who are in the majority. Corn Countians take it for granted that they live in a Christian society. It was thought desirable, therefore, to ascertain, if possible, what was thought distinctive about the Christian faith.

2. *The Meaning of Easter*

Of the major events in Christian history whose meaning is determinative for the belief structure and for the determination of devotion and action, Easter would, presumably, be accorded primary importance. It was, therefore, decided to ascertain what understandings prevailed about the meaning of this unique event in Christian life and thought.

3. *The Nature of God*

Among an almost unanimously theistic people there are

assumptions about the nature of God and the way man is related to the Supreme Being. Men may define God in an infinite number of ways, and any one person may find it necessary to resort to numerous definitions as no particular one seems adequate. An attempt to give a definition at least brings to the fore some of the dominant feelings one may have about the nature of God. It should be added that, as was the case with all the other queries, the inquiry presumes no one response to be normative or the best. Rather, the concern was to get as accurate and comprehensive a picture as possible of the general thought about the nature of God.

Following the three questions that it was believed would reflect some basic theological foundations, Corn Countians were also asked under what circumstances they thought people were most likely to be religious and why they thought people engaged in prayer. Worship, broadly conceived, is the principal function of religion, and prayer is the center of worship. Church life centers around the act of worship. For this reason it seemed justifiable to ascertain what this phase of church life meant in so far as words could be found to express that meaning.

In the world contest for the loyalty of men and nations, much is made of the fact that theistic and atheistic systems are in conflict. It was thought worth-while to discover how deep are roots and how grounded in theistic beliefs are the ultimate loyalties of Corn Countians.

DISTINCTIVENESS OF CHRISTIANITY

The question was asked of each person, "If you were talking with someone who was not a Christian and he asked you what was special or distinctive about your religion, that is, about Jesus and Christianity, what would you say?"

Obviously, not everyone who found himself unable to make an answer was actually totally uninformed or unfamiliar with the uniqueness of the Christian faith. It is significant, however, that a sizable percentage found themselves unable to articulate anything that might characterize Christianity's uniqueness. In Main Town, 42 per cent of the Protestants were at a loss for an answer, while in River Town the number among the Protestants reached 45 per cent and in Serviceville 40 per cent. In the open country the record among Protestants was slightly better—34 per cent.

The Catholic response in Main Town was identical with the Protestant, but in River Town their awareness of any distinctiveness about Christianity reached a high of 57 per cent.

Pursuant to the work of Horace Bushnell and the conscious focus upon character development in religious education, the curriculums of so-called "liberal" churches stressed the importance of the character of Jesus and of the necessity to try to grow into his likeness. The Character Education Movement and the Religious Education Association paralleled and reinforced each other's efforts and gained substantial support shortly after the beginning of this century. Each emphasized the close relation between the outstanding personalities of Hebrew-Christian history and contemporary personal integrity. It is now commonly known history that some theological seminaries participating actively in the social gospel movement produced among their students a vigorous social-ethical concern. This concern stemmed in no small measure from the desire to remake individuals and society after the exemplary qualities of Jesus.

It was, therefore, of some interest to discern to what extent this injunction to "live like Jesus" and to appropriate literally his teachings found expression in present-day church members.

Whether the same disillusionment befell Corn Countians which later came to the centers of theological education, over the seeming impossibility of patterning one's life after the example of Jesus, would be difficult to ascertain. The fact is that only a very small per cent of Corn Countians suggest that Christianity's distinctiveness lies in Jesus' exemplary character. On the other hand, with the exception of River Town, well over half of the respondents attribute Christianity's distinctiveness to theological characteristics of its central figure. These would include such replies as "He was the Son of God," "We're saved because of Him," or "He was perfect."

It might be hypothesized that the churches stressing a more liturgical-type service could be expected to have their replies more heavily weighted on the side of theological explanation. Similarly, the Presbyterians, with at least a modest measure of familiarity with the theological system of John Calvin, might be expected to reply in that vein. On the contrary, the two Lutheran bodies and the Presbyterians are among the lowest in theological response. Perhaps this is compensated in the Presbyterian instance by the fact that their responses under the "exemplary" category is the very highest (Table 7).

Nor is it surprising that persons with above-average intelligence led both in the theological weighting of their replies and in their suggestions that an advantage of Christianity lay in the commendable qualities of its principal figure.

Obviously, a Corn Countian is not in a religiously competitive situation with non-Christian religions. However

TABLE 7. *Distinctive Aspects of Christianity in Per Cent for Selected Denominations—Main Town*

Church Membership of Respondent	N=	Distinctive Element Cited: Role of Jesus: Theological	Role of Jesus: Exemplary	All Religions the Same	No Substantive Response: "Never Discuss Religion"	No Substantive Response: Response Does not Answer Question	No Substantive Response: "Don't know"
Baptist	44	71	16	0	5	5	27
Catholic	52	62	1	8	17	15	10
Christian	20	75	15	0	5	5	25
Congregational	73	73	8	1	1	4	15
Lutheran, Augustana	42	64	7	2	7	12	17
Lutheran, United	81	47	12	3	11	14	22
Methodist	82	65	9	1	2	16	11
Mission Covenant	54	83	9	0	4	11	9
Presbyterian	44	50	23	5	11	11	14
None	111	48	19	1	3	11	25

much he may be admonished that the truest criterion of the Christian faith is the extent of its witnesses, he is not under compulsion to justify his faith against some other. The things for which his forebears strived are now attained. He has a measure of security in the comforts at hand but even more in the assurance that governmental leaders can regulate the economic system and international relations so that human welfare is protected. He has not been confronted with the necessity of choosing between well-defined rival systems. In other words, there is no crisis. Ostensibly, nothing he might do could have a bearing on the contest between the international titans each theoretically representing a diametrically opposite faith. This contest is going on thousands of miles away even though videotape may report uprisings based on these conflicting faiths within minutes after their ocurrence. One can only conclude that the essence or content of the Christian faith is not a pressing and dynamic concern of Corn Countians.

THE MEANING OF EASTER

It is assumed that without Easter there would have been no Christianity. There would seem to be general agreement among those most sensitive to the importance and meaning of the Christian faith that it is God's action in the resurrection that distinguishes Christianity from all other religions. This is not to imply that the resurrection was a single act. It is, however, to contend that the Spirit of Christ lived on after the crucifixion and continues to exist even now. This, presumably, is the meaning of the "Living Christ."

If the results of the inquiry can be relied upon, there is a great deal of fuzziness and uncertainty among church people concerning the central act of their faith. The broad range of responses included everything from the coming of spring to "proof that Jesus was God." This range would, of course, include the idea of immortality. Some identified it as the time of the death of Christ and a few others as the occasion of the birth of Christ. Most common is the response that it was the occasion of the resurrection. An unusually high percentage of nonchurch members appear in the "Don't know" column. Next to the resurrection interpretation, as might be expected, were the replies that included the idea of immortality or the identification of the religious event with the breaking forth of new life in nature.

The uncertainty that Protestants feel about Easter and its significance is reflected in their responses under the category of reformulative effort. (By this is meant the desire to find a formula that accommodates several interpretations.) Approximately one fourth of each denomination seeks to find some way of correlating the total significance of that event with the generally conceived doctrines of immortality and the seasonal variation. The exception to this, and a very sharp exception, is found among the Congregationalists, who apparently have almost twice as much concern about the reformulation of Easter's meaning (44 per cent). (Table 8.) On the other hand, that denomination is at the lowest point of those who give a conventional interpretation based on the concept of the resurrection (43 per cent). Highest in the list of those who give the conventional explanation are the members of the Mission Covenant church (76 per cent). Actually the spread between the respective denominations in this regard is not great.

Theology has been designated historically as the queen of the sciences. From it the meaning and purpose of all other scientific disciplines are seen in perspective and their results evaluated. It provides the ultimate norms against which ideas and events are appraised. This is not to say that there is only one theology. Of course there are many, and among Christian theologians there is a broad spectrum along which any man's particular theology will be found. Easter is one of those primary events in the history of our faith that calls out responses all along the spectrum. One interviewee may have unwittingly expressed some of the

TABLE 8. *The Meaning of Easter in Per Cent for Selected Denominations—Main Town*

CHURCH MEMBERSHIP OF RESPONDENT	N=	MEANING CITED						
		Descriptive		*Theological*				
		Resurrection of Jesus	Other	Traditional or classical	Reformulative effort	*Negative*	*Other*	*"Don't know"*
Baptist	44	61	2	25	23	0	14	9
Catholic	52	69	6	15	17	0	15	6
Christian	20	60	0	20	5	2	20	5
Congregational	73	43	1	15	44	8	12	10
Lutheran, Augustana	42	74	12	26	26	0	5	5
Lutheran, United	81	52	10	16	20	0	11	19
Methodist	82	51	6	27	24	7	12	4
Mission Covenant	54	76	6	20	24	0	13	2
Presbyterian	44	52	11	23	27	5	18	7
None	111	34	5	10	12	14	15	21

dilemma of the theologian concerning Easter when she, repeating a speech mannerism that prefaced everything she said (everything was "more or less"), announced that for her Easter was the time when "Jesus more or less arose."

The meaning of Easter is so completely tied with questions of history, mythology, magic, and faith that no single interpretation is uniformly accepted. The ultimate meaning, therefore, derives from the theological perspective with which one views and accepts the events of Easter. To some persons of limited intellectual capacity, the physical resurrection may present no basis for doubt. On the other hand, to a scientifically trained person, the physical resurrection may present basis for extensive doubt. At the same time, to many individuals possessed of superior intellectual capacity and training, the resurrection presents no cause for doubt but rather affirmation and devotion.

Among Corn Countians there was an obvious increase in capacity for comprehending the more profound meanings of Easter on the part of persons in the above-average intelligence levels. More than five times as many in the above-average group sought to find expression for the meaning of the event in something that was more nearly consistent with their intellectual patterns. It would seem possible to conclude, therefore, that there is a desire on the part of the more thoughtful church members for some comprehension of the meaning of Easter that makes possible the combined use of their capacities for both faith and reason. This is not to be construed as derogatory of those who gave the habitual or catechized response. It does point up again, though, the ever-recurring question of the means for interpreting the basic elements of the Christian faith to persons of widely varying intellectual capacities.

THE NATURE OF GOD

Theology is the study of the nature of God and the formulation of beliefs about God. It is hardly to be expected that lay people would give well-thought-out and comprehensive answers to the question, "If a child should ask you what is God like, what would you say?" Nevertheless, every phase of church participation is posited on the existence and the nature of God. Much of our community life takes this for granted, and the origins and present-day conduct of the affairs of the nation are posited on the existence of a Supreme Being. Few seem to have given much thought to the nature of this Being and even fewer have attempted to formulate their thoughts in any consistent fashion.

Most prominent by a substantial margin was the characterization of God by attributes—that is, as a spirit, love, kindness, governor of the universe, eternal, perfect, judge, forgiving. Of this group, however, the idea of God as creator or as judge are only very rarely mentioned. Foremost in the scale were the attributes of love and spirit. It is interesting that there is little variation in this from community to community and between Protestant and Catholic.

An almost complete avoidance of any suggestion that God presented a judgmental aspect may be worthy of investigation (approximately 2 per cent). In a large measure the responses assume God to possess a benign nature. The question cannot but arise whether only catastrophe resulting from man's violation of God's demands as seen in human history can inspire or instill any recognition of judgment as an integral characteristic of the Supreme Being. Perhaps another way of asking the same question would be to request the respondent to define sin and its consequences. Unfortunately, the inquiry made no attempt to explore the meaning of sin as understood by Corn Countians. Had this been done, it might have suggested more of the judgmental aspect of God.

The second most common category for response was that which incorporated the traditional characterization, i.e., Supreme Being, omnipresent, all powerful or all knowing.

Two other categories, each substantially below those just referred to, are: the analogical (God is like a father); and the quasi-anthropomorphic (watching over you). It may be a source of some reassurance that the popular characterization "the Man upstairs" begets only a very slight response, but, even so, it has a slight edge over the idea of God as Father.

Aside from the Baptists and Disciples at the low end of the scale in traditional characterization, and the Catholics at the high end, there is little difference between the respective denominations (Table 9). When it comes to the range as characterized by attributes, the Congregationalists are lowest and the Mission Covenant highest, with the Presbyterians second highest.

It would naturally be asked whether those denominations with the greatest emphasis upon a liturgical service and catechetical training might tend to respond strongly in

TABLE 9. *Characterization of God in Per Cent for Selected Denominations—Main Town*

CHURCH MEMBERSHIP OF RESPONDENT	N=	CHARACTERIZATION OF GOD						
		Traditional Characterization	*Analogical*	*Quasi-anthropomorphic*	*Characterized by Attributes*	*Quasi-psychological*	*Other*	*"Don't know"*
Baptist	44	11	20	7	68	9	18	34
Catholic	52	50	4	12	60	10	15	10
Christian	20	10	20	5	45	15	5	30
Congregational	73	34	12	8	44	18	12	16
Lutheran, Augustana	42	33	7	14	62	7	14	17
Lutheran, United	81	26	14	5	46	19	14	24
Methodist	82	28	13	11	55	13	17	16
Mission Covenant	54	24	30	11	87	6	7	9
Presbyterian	44	34	23	11	75	9	11	14
None	111	14	6	6	38	14	20	31

traditional terms or in classifications that are most commonly used where the Deity is described. This is not borne out by the data, with the exception of the Catholics. The latter, in company with the Mission Covenant members, are lowest in the scale of those who indicated inability to make any characterization of God.

And again, as was true in previous instances, the number of persons capable of describing the characteristics of the Deity increased with the increase of intellectual ability—there being approximately a 100 per cent increase between the below-average and above-average respondent. These differences are substantially greater than the differences between denominations, with the interesting exception that one of the denominations possessing a substantially larger number of members with above average intelligence, the Congregationalists, is, as was indicated, lowest in the characterization of God by attributes. And again, as has been true of other areas analyzed, the United Lutherans differed only insignificantly in per cent. Here a liturgical church and a so-called nonliturgical church with a long history of educational emphasis are composed equally of individuals only moderately capable or desirous of characterizing the Supreme Being. Whether this is the result of totally opposite reasons of course would be difficult to determine. May it be that the uncertainties and theological vaguenesses that characterize contemporary society are also reflected in these two denominations, however different in their patterns of worship?

Protestant women seem much more likely than Protestant men to characterize God by attributes. Since the question was phrased with the possibility that it might be an answer given to a child, the superior capacity of women to reach the mind of the child may account for this more vivid and less theoretical reply. Men may lack experience in transposing theoretical concepts into understandable analogies.

That there is no one overriding interpretation of the nature of God is, of course, not surprising. To some extent the varying religious traditions, but even more the leveling influence of popular assumption and understandings, have exercised their effect. One suspects that the latter is the dominant influence at present.

EXPRESSING RELIGION

Very few people would agree on an identical interpretation of the meaning of the word "religious." Nevertheless, religion is a phenomenon among every people however primitive or sophisticated. Few would deny, for example, that the American people are overwhelmingly religious, basing the opinion on church attendance, popular songs, public oaths, etc. The manner in which they exhibit religion may run all the way from perfunctorily singing "God Bless America" to the voluntarily accepted self-discipline of an organization making great demands upon one's time, money, and belief. Measured by this latter criterion, the communists are profoundly religious.

This fact puzzles Americans because we have been led to believe that the elite group that dominates Russian thought and action is irreligious. All of this points up the fact that we are hazy about differences between religions and about what is durable and ultimate concerning our own, whatever name it might be given.

As is true of all the previous areas of exploration, and likewise of those which follow, there is no evidence that serious thought has been applied to the range or content of what is commonly regarded as religious. The means used for discerning what the term connotes to most people was to ask the question, "Under what circumstances do you think a person is most religious?"

The preponderance of replies to this question incorporate reference to death and illness and the apprehension that accompanies the imminence or presence of each. An almost complete absence of any suggestion that a full expression of religion might consist of one's giving of himself to others, as an act comparable to or in appreciation of God's gift to us, indicates something about our teaching of religion. The mystery of death and the eagerness to be extricated from suffering are certainly an identifiable aspect of religion. But that the replies should deal almost exclusively with those areas may provide some clues as to why those interested in the total welfare of society have found it so difficult to bring the forces of religion to bear upon the common welfare. Quickly it should be added that the respondents may have had in mind the response to human need as well as the feeling of it which could be identified as religious. Those who replied that at the time of personal need was religion most likely to be experienced are substantially more numerous than those who insisted that death prompted the largest religious concern. The fact, too, that the persons of above-average intelligence related religion to need in more than twice the degree than did those possessing below-average intellectual ability might indicate that the fuller range in the idea of need was included in their understanding of what was religious. However, the fact remains that there is almost no reference to the meeting of need by the individual as a form of religious expression. Neither is there a suggestion that living out of gratitude for God's goodness or knowing the recipience of forgiveness plays any particular part in being religious.

REASONS FOR PRAYER

Petition

With the interpretation of religion being what it is as described above, one might well expect that the forms undertaken for relating one's self to the Deity would fall largely within those categories, and they do. Petition and feeling of dependence are given as the two main reasons for engaging in prayer. The next two categories, but by no means serious competitors for even near ranking, are forgiveness and thanksgiving.

Since religion, to so many of the respondents, was at its height during times of need it would be natural that petition to have that need answered would loom largest in the uses for prayer. To this, however, must be added the desire to resolve the deeper anxieties of the human spirit and the longing to find some certitude of direction. For a considerable number desiring to know the fulfillment of this life in some less troubled and more perfect existence, prayer was the instrument for facilitating one's getting to heaven.

Dependence

To a very substantial number, prayer provides a sense of intimacy and dependence which gives reassurance and a sense of being cared for. Next to petition, this response came second. This would seem to be both understandable and commendable if, as a result of familiarity with the Scriptures through the years, one has come to recognize that in and of himself he is not complete—that his own life is of importance beyond itself. Whether these same individuals who attach so large an importance to this dependence and trust are also the ones who assume responsibility for the rest of God's creation we cannot say.

Forgiveness

As has been indicated earlier, sin does not constitute a heavy weight upon the consciousness of Corn Countians, so the request for forgiveness appears but infrequently. No denomination numbered among its respondents as many as one fifth who included forgiveness as a part of their prayer practice.

Thanksgiving

This form of prayer finds a rather impressive number of practitioners. Approximately one third of the Presbyterians, Mission Covenanters, and Roman Catholics indicate that for them thanksgiving is one of the principal reasons for prayer. This does not mean that they did not include other things as well, but at least they did include thanksgiving. It is interesting to note by way of comparison that no Presbyterians expressed the need for forgiveness, but at least they are thankful. The Congregationalists are slightly in need of forgiveness (8 per cent), and are thankful in exactly the same measure. Here again, only the United Lutherans are lower in the sense of need for forgiveness.

There were many other categories, including a rather small "Don't know" column, but few of these reached as high as 10 per cent, so they are not included in the specific designation.

In a comparison of the denominations as a whole there is no great difference between them in the reasons expressed by their members as impelling them to engage in prayer. Noteworthy is the fact that the so-called liturgical churches seem to beget no greater participation in the full extent and meaning of prayer than do those whose emphasis is on other aspects of church life.

It must be assumed that other influences than theological

foundations and ecclesiastical traditions are shaping and informing the prayer life and that which impels it. Whether this is because the historical traditions of the several churches and the emphases they are now making are insufficient, or whether the incentives and rationale for prayer are distorted by other forces must remain in the realm of conjecture.

CHAPTER VII

CHURCH MEMBERS AND PUBLIC DECISIONS

A DESCRIPTION of any conscious relation between Christian faith and major social issues as understood by Corn Countians can be brief. Any adequate analysis of the reasons for the present state of this relationship would, however, be long and complex and does not come within the scope of this study.

Almost all the denominations represented in Corn County have employed staffs whose chief purpose is to acquaint the constituents of their denomination with the relevance of the Christian faith to major social issues and to increase the support of church members for constructive action. In addition, theological seminaries related to most of the denominations here involved, or which train men for these several denominations, give much attention to the problems of religion in ethical action. The seminary graduates serving the churches of Corn County are men who would represent a fair cross section of theological seminary graduates for the country at large. This is an off-the-cuff judgment based on personal acquaintance with most of the men serving churches in the communities studied. That their parishioners exhibited no particular interest in the connection between social issues and their personal faith can hardly be attributed to unique deficiencies in the training or professional service of their ministers. The roots lie more deeply in the culture and the common experience of our times.

More pressing in the minds of those conducting the study was the desire to secure a general picture of the reaction on the part of these respondents to some issues and themes about which there is wide difference and often strong variation in response. Historically, for example, the Midwest has been the center of isolationist support prior to World Wars I and II. Recognizing this, Franklin D. Roosevelt came to the Midwest to deliver his "Quarantine the Aggressor" speech. Sentiment against the League of Nations after World War I was strong, as reflected by the newspaper with the largest circulation in the region.

THE UNITED NATIONS

With this in mind the respondents were asked for their opinion about the United Nations, since it was assumed that this might afford a reasonable index of isolationism or international co-operation. With the exception of Serviceville, each of the communities gave overwhelming support to the United Nations. Serviceville presents something of a puzzle —it has the lowest measure of approval (Catholics, 41 per cent; Protestants, 59 per cent) and the highest percentage of disapproval, but it also presents the largest percentage of those church members whose responses are registered in the "Don't know" column. The fact that Serviceville is on no main highway and has no industry or employing organization that would bring people in and out of the community may serve to explain in some measure the apparent obstruction in flow of ideas. However, the open country townships around Serviceville present, curiously, the highest percentage of favorable response to the United Nations and, correspondingly, the lowest disapproval and the fewest who "Don't know." Though the Catholics, for example, in Serviceville register the lowest approval, the Catholics in the open country attending the same church (Serviceville) represent the highest percentage of approval. One possible inference to draw from this is the fact that Catholics living in the open country represent a higher economic and intelligence level and are more conversant with the major trends in contemporary life. It may also be hypothesized that both Catholics and Protestants living on farms are aware of the fact that American agriculture is inescapably tied to world markets and that the future of the farm problem lies in a large measure with the ability to resolve the international problem.

Looking at the response of all denominations in Main Town to the United Nations, we find no sharply discernible pattern of differentiation. In Main Town the Catholic approval is close to the highest, and those who "Don't know" are among the lowest. It would appear that, as in so many other instances, the factors making for near uniformity are other than those inherent within the denominational emphasis. It perhaps should be noted again that the two Swedish-background churches present the largest number of persons who are unfamiliar with the problem and who are also lowest in approval of the UN. It will be remembered that these are the two denominations with the best record of Biblical familiarity.

It would appear, then, that there is a strong and widespread desire to use an instrument as widely publicized and already proven as the UN to achieve and guarantee peace. The fact that the UN places upon our shores so large a number of representatives from other nations seems not to be a source of apprehension. Whether church affiliation or theological reasoning can be accredited with any measure of this UN approval cannot, of course, be known. It may well be that a desire for peace prompted by and based upon religious presuppositions is responsible for the very substantial approval of church members. Without any reference made to a religious motivation for it, the approval cannot be specifically credited to that source. Because of the considerable uniformity, one must infer that the widespread news about the UN's effectiveness and the extensive coverage of the various sessions provided by both radio and television in addition to the press have served to build a confidence in the UN as a means of fulfilling the best interests of the United States in the deliberations and contests involving other nations. Likewise, the stanch resistance registered to the activities of the Soviet Union might have fostered additional enthusiasm for the agency.

In the light of responses by church people to other issues involving collective action, one cannot but conclude that official action by churches and education for decision based upon theological foundations are not prominent. Unconsciously perhaps, church people may assume that political agencies are serving the ends and objectives for society that their faith would encourage and sustain. Perhaps this is the most that can be expected for the time being or for the future. Protestants seem to have little conception of the way in which organizations might serve to fulfill the deep longings in matters of the public good which the Christian faith would seem to call for. In a matter, for example, as universally important as world peace might it be possible for church leaders to make much more explicit the role of institutions and organizations in fulfilling the long-range desires on the part of church participants. In the interviewing among Roman Catholics the pattern was consistently repetitive, as expressed by the respondents, namely, that Catholics do not engage in political activity. Those Catholics interviewed at least were convinced that their church dealt primarily with spiritual matters. They were almost completely unaware of any organization such as the National Catholic Welfare Conference and the Organization of Bishops, whereby the objectives of the church are made known at points where influence can be exerted. Protestants, though, in the very nature of their type of ecclesiastical structure, are dependent upon an informed constituency, and with their opinions grounded in theological foundations are presumably under obligation to relate themselves informedly and conscientiously to the issues of society. Obviously this is not a commonly held assumption on the part of Corn Countians. Responsibility for decisions affecting the well-being of society seems to lie elsewhere than in the church and its people.

LABOR UNIONS

From their inception, labor unions have been an object of mystery and often of suspicion on the part of some church people, both Protestant and Catholic. Any assembly of individuals organized to exercise power and to use force if necessary to accomplish economic objectives has seemingly been inconsistent with the nonviolence and the turning-of-the-other-cheek emphasis characteristic of church teachings. In addition to this contradiction of teaching was the fact that the labor movement was largely an urban phenomenon and the largest percentage of its adherents were not church members in the middle-class brackets. They were frequently immigrants and represented a stratum of society unknown to a large body of American people who, though in an industrializing nation, were themselves still very close to rural roots.

The great depression of the 1930's changed much of this. Agriculture had been in a depression for a decade prior to the depression of the 1930's. Agriculture had already begun the processes of organization to secure by collective action the ends that it sought from government. Therefore, agriculture and rurally oriented people were not as hostile to labor as previously when the National Labor Relations Act of 1935 was enacted. With the uniform prosperity of industry and agriculture during and pursuant to World War II, any ideological differences were kept well in the background. Perhaps because labor was more tightly organized and more sensitive to economic forces, it took the initiative in attempting to tell agriculture that the destinies and welfare of agriculture and labor were inseparably intertwined. Industry, on the other hand, felt called upon to remind the farmer that he was primarily a businessman. The honeymoon between agriculture and labor was short-lived. The largest farm organization supported the Taft-Hartley Act of 1948, many of whose sponsors sought to place limits upon or reduce the gains of labor. Subsequently, still another major effort was made to limit the power of labor through the institution of right-to-work laws. Of the eighteen states adopting this form of legislation, most were primarily rural.

This sketchy review of the relationships between rural people and the development of organized labor is cited to illustrate something of the traditional attitudes prevailing between these two major groups in our economic and political life. Corn County, being predominantly agricultural, has relatively few members of the labor movement. It does, on the other hand, have a very strong contingent active in organized farm life. It was, therefore, deemed advisable to ascertain whether the shifting roles of the two great organized blocs—agriculture and labor—had markedly conditioned the thinking of Corn Countians about organized labor and organized agriculture. More will be said of the latter in the next section.

One metropolitan daily which comes to Main Town outsells all other newspapers combined. It is, itself, a widely recognized symbol of conservatism. The county newspaper published in Main Town likewise takes pride in its conservatism. It claims for itself the distinction of being the largest paper of its kind in the country and unquestionably it blankets the county.

Therefore, with this combined impact of conservative thought plus the traditional rural suspicion of organized labor, it was hypothesized that the people of the county would be at least somewhat cool toward organized labor. At the time some of the interviewing was in progress, national attention was being focused on abuses in the labor movement; and all the media of communication carried the accounts, since the hearings were of a highly sensational nature. Despite this fact, the clean-cut approval of labor unions was rather high (Table 10). If "qualified approval" is added to the clean-cut approval, the general sympathy for labor unions is overwhelming. The column "Qualified Approval" had to be introduced because so many persons

TABLE 10. *Attitude Toward Labor Unions in Per Cent for Selected Denominations—Main Town*

CHURCH MEMBERSHIP OF RESPONDENT	N=	ATTITUDE INDICATED			
		Approval	*Disapproval*	*Qualified Approval*	*"Don't know"*
Baptist	43	28	14	37	21
Catholic	49	41	12	41	6
Christian	20	20	15	45	20
Congregational	70	24	7	53	16
Lutheran, Augustana	40	15	18	40	28
Lutheran, United	78	21	18	42	19
Methodist	79	24	14	53	9
Mission Covenant	53	28	9	40	23
Presbyterian	43	12	16	58	14
None	105	41	15	30	14

replied in almost identical words: "Labor unions are all right but they have gone too far." Presumably, the hearings had a substantial effect.

The highest percentage of approval comes from River Town, with a background of labor organizations in coal mining, and in the factories of the town just over the county line and adjacent to River Town. The lowest percentage of approval is found among the farm residents in the open country; but here again, when coupled with those giving qualified approval, it adds up to very substantial support. Again it is in Serviceville, the off-the-main-road town, where there is the highest percentage of disapproval of labor and the highest percentage of those who feel they are unfamiliar with the problem.

The lowest percentage of approval comes from the Presbyterians, but, significantly, they likewise represent the highest percentage of those giving qualified approval. This perhaps can be construed as begrudging acknowledgment on the part of a church in the high status brackets for intelligence, income, and education that what has taken place in the reorganization of the power structure might just as well be accepted. It should be noted that the Congregationalists and Methodists are almost identical with each other and only slightly behind the Presbyterians in their negative reactions.

Women are somewhat less ready to approve labor unions, and they appear substantially more numerous in the "Don't know" column. Where attitude toward unions is correlated with intelligence, the above-average group gives approval in only 50 per cent of the measure of those who are below average but 100 per cent more inclined to give qualified approval than their below-average brethren.

FARMERS ORGANIZATIONS

The major farm organization of Corn County does not insist that its members be bona fide farmers. Therefore, persons who have an interest in agriculture and who wish to register their desire through a pressure group find this organization a very active and powerful pressure group.

As indicated above, farm organizations, though marked by sporadic efforts, with accomplishments and defeats paralleling the labor movement, did discover that they had to provide services in addition to being ideological rallying points if they were to hold their members. Thus it was not until the farm organizations developed insurance programs, co-operative purchasing and marketing programs, and large-scale educational activities that they were enabled to hold their constituency. Labor, correspondingly, had to develop the check-off and to provide innumerable personal services both within and outside the plant to keep its membership from receding in critical times. These policies have served to maintain a stable membership, even while supporting philosophies about which the members may have misgivings. Whatever those misgivings may be, there is at least the common assumption that the pressure group as a whole is attempting to do something constructive about the agricultural dilemma. This it would seem might account for the extraordinary degree of approval of farm organizations. Only 2 per cent of the Catholics and 6 per cent of the Protestants expressed disapproval.

With its three new factories and several older ones, Main Town has an overtone of industrial life despite the fact that it is the county seat of an agricultural county. This presumably explains why approximately one fourth of the respondents indicated that they were unfamiliar with the problem of farmer organizations.

In River Town, with its emphasis almost entirely in the direction of industry and commerce, a sizable percentage indicate their unfamiliarity with the problem. In both Serviceville and the open country, the favorable disposition toward farm organizations can be reasonably understood. There is only very slight variation in the attitudes registered by the members of the several denominations, and the differences between those of the respective intelligence levels are of little significance.

Farm organizations, it would appear, are highly acceptable, and the principal of exercising pressure through agencies which serve to stabilize the economy and to give some guarantees of wholesome economic life are acceptable. Here again the fact that there is no difference to be noted between denominations would suggest that theological distinctions are hardly determinative in making economic judgments.

SOCIAL SECURITY

Traditionally, rural people have been ruggedly independent. As the depression of the 1930's worsened, the reluctance of rural people to accept assistance declined. Eventually came the realization that the problems afflicting the nation and the world could not be defeated by individual ruggedness, and that these same problems were created in a large measure by the very nature of our technology and the economic system we have chosen. This awakening, apparently, became one of the watersheds in modern history. The realization that human beings were inevitably the victims of a system they had created provided a shock of unprecedented nature. Pride in individual accomplishment and the expectation of yet greater achievements had to succumb to the facts of an industrial society. The alternative was a completely managed and authoritarian economic order. It was this bowing to reality which made for a reversal in attitude toward accepting assistance.

The passing of the Social Security Act of 1935 and its subsequent retention by every succeeding administration in the national Government and the absence of any serious denunciation of the act constitutes one of the indexes of attitudinal change on the part of even those who had historically been opposed to accepting aid.

Because of the quality of its agriculture, the high investment in machinery per capita, and the comparatively large productivity per farm, Midwestern agriculture was in a substantially different position from that of those areas of the nation which could produce only a small fraction of agricultural products despite a large number of farms. The commercial aspect of agriculture which characterizes the traditional family farm of the Midwest understandably served to identify family farmers with the business community. Nevertheless, with the prolonged depression in agriculture, beginning almost a decade before the industrial depression, the agricultural community of the Midwest found itself kindly disposed toward the development of social security. Though no polling of Corn Countians for attitudes toward an insurance program such as the Social Security Act represents was taken prior to the great depression, there was widespread and frequent expression on the part of Corn Countians to the effect that they never expected they "would come to this." They see nothing wrong with it now.

The present inquiry among Corn Countians relative to social security reveals overwhelming approval. It might have been even greater if the sample reported, instead of including the ages thirty to sixty-four, included those above that age. In the actual interviewing, in response to the query, "Are you in favor of social security?" the reply very frequently was: "Why not? I'm getting it."

As between the denominations, if qualified approval is added to outright and full approval the responses reach almost 90 per cent for every denomination. In no denomination did disapproval among the members reach as high as 10 per cent. The sharpest differentiation is that between the persons of below-average and above-average intellectual ability. The latter express about 25 per cent less enthusiasm, but here again, when their qualifications are taken into account, their degree of approval is almost identical with those below average in intellectual ability (87 per cent vs. 89 per cent). Presumably, individuals of somewhat superior intelligence recognize certain of the dangers involved in a universal welfare coverage and register their protest in the form of a reservation but actually suspect there is no viable alternative.

FEDERAL HEALTH INSURANCE

With rising medical costs and the proliferation of health insurance programs and the corresponding denunciation of these programs by medical and other organizations, it was thought that a portrayal of contemporary attitudes in this much-debated issue might be helpful. When responses were received to the inquiry concerning social security, it seemed desirable to ascertain whether attitudes toward these related issues might resemble each other.

There was markedly less interest in or approval of Federal health insurance than for social security. Table 11 indicates the response to the query concerning Federal health insurance. Approval, for the most part, is less than 50 per cent and among the Protestants in the open country it dropped to 25 per cent.

Why does there seem to be so little ambiguity or uncertainty about social security on the part of the people in all the communities studied and yet a comparatively high degree of uncertainty about the issue of Federal health insurance? It runs as high as 36 per cent among the Catholics of River Town and 35 per cent each among the non-church people of Main Town and River Town.

Whatever accounts for 56 per cent of the Protestants and 43 per cent of the Catholics in the open country registering disapproval of health insurance gives cause for conjecture.

TABLE 11. *Attitude Toward Federal Health Insurance in Per Cent by Broad Membership Groups and Residential Areas*

CHURCH MEMBERSHIP OF RESPONDENT	N=	ATTITUDE INDICATED		
		Approval	*Disapproval*	*"Don't know"*
		Main Town		
Catholic	51	51	35	14
Protestant	463	30	43	27
None	59	31	34	35
		River Town		
Catholic	100	42	22	36
Protestant	82	45	38	17
None	46	50	15	35
		Serviceville		
Catholic	22	59	23	18
Protestant	132	39	39	22
None	31	39	35	26
		Open Country		
Catholic	14	36	43	21
Protestant	63	25	56	19
None	31	48	32	20

Is this a vestigial remnant of the hostility toward regimentation or an outburst of protest on behalf of such individualism as can yet be expressed? Or is it the result of effective and extensive propaganda? It is interesting that the response of farmers in registering disapproval against Federal health insurance is the highest in any of the communities, and this is true for both Catholics and Protestants.

In the interviewing, among those registering approval, there came to be an almost uniform and standard response to the query, "What is your opinion of Federal health insurance?" Many who indicated they were in favor of it added quickly, "providing you don't mean socialized medicine." It became apparent that whatever groups were having access to the minds of Corn Countians had done a successful piece of work in building up resistance to "socialized medicine." The interviewers of necessity had to record the replies as approval because the approval was given to "Federal health insurance." Possibly the use of the terms "Federal" and "insurance" gained for the total concept a measure of favorable disposition.

Among the respective denominations, the Presbyterians registered the highest percentage of disapproval, with the Congregationalists next in order (Table 12). As has been suggested frequently heretofore, these are the two denominations with the highest percentage of middle- and upper-status constituents. The lowest percentage of approval was registered by the Mission Covenant constituents, but they also registered the highest percentage of those who were unfamiliar with the issue (47 per cent). On the other hand, the highest degree of approval was recorded by the Catholics, and they in turn revealed the lowest percentage of those who appear in the "Don't know" column. The reason

TABLE 12. *Attitude Toward Federal Health Insurance in Per Cent for Selected Denominations—Main Town*

CHURCH MEMBERSHIP OF RESPONDENT	N=	ATTITUDE INDICATED		
		Approval	*Disapproval*	*"Don't know"*
Baptist	43	26	44	30
Catholic	51	51	35	14
Christian	19	32	53	15
Congregational	65	35	49	16
Lutheran, Augustana	41	29	42	29
Lutheran, United	77	31	42	27
Methodist	74	30	43	27
Mission Covenant	54	20	33	47
Presbyterian	41	22	58	20
None	59	31	34	35

for this is uncertain. It can be hypothesized, however, that Catholics are less accustomed to independent action in their religious life and that action which is taken by central authorities (*Federal* health insurance) has a greater likelihood of approval. In River Town, however, the Catholic approval was only 42 per cent, but even so, this was almost twice the degree of disapproval. In this town and in this particular denomination, with so large a number of those in the middle- and lower-class brackets, there was the highest percentage of response in the "Don't know" column. Protestant men are substantially more inclined to disapprove Federal health insurance than Protestant women (53 per cent vs. 37 per cent). Where intellectual ability is the variable, persons above average are more inclined to disapprove than those below (55 per cent vs. 37 per cent). And when considering the blue-collar–white-collar analysis the difference is even greater, with 60 per cent of the white-collar respondents disapproving, as against 33 per cent of the blue-collar.

A review of the data relative to Federal health insurance would indicate that though the greater strength is registered on the disapproval side, there is a substantial percentage of respondents who either have not yet made up their minds or feel that they do not know enough about the issue to make a response. This group is largest among the non-church members, those of below-average intelligence and who are blue-collar workers.

DENOMINATIONS AND SOCIAL ISSUES

If one were seeking a clue to whether church constituents regard their denomination at the national level as important in the influencing of public policy or the general welfare, this portion of the study would seem to provide it. Preliminary acquaintance with Corn Countians had led to the hypothesis that expressions of denominational concern for social issues are not regarded as indispensable or even very significant by members of local churches. Denominations, therefore, seem to serve a purpose quite other than that of being the conscience of local churches and their people. Despite frequent protests of loyalty and genuine enthusiasm for the denomination, this particular phase of its life figures insignificantly.

The question was asked of each respondent, "Do you know of any social issues on which your denomination has taken a stand?" With the exception of the Catholics in Main Town, more than 75 per cent of the respondents had no knowledge of any position that their respective denomination had taken on any social issue. Correspondingly, the low percentage of those who had a knowledge of at least one issue reveals less than 25 per cent in this category with the exception of the Catholics in Main Town, of whom 40 per cent had some knowledge. This can be explained, possibly, by the fact that the Catholics in Main Town seemed to be aware of their church's stand on communism.

Protestant unawareness ranged from 100 per cent on the part of the United Lutherans to 67 per cent for the Methodists (Table 13). The latter denomination's members seemed predominantly aware of a historic stand against alcoholic beverages. Approximately one fifth of the Baptists and Mission Covenant members possessed some familiarity with an issue of concern to the denomination as a whole. It might be hypothesized that the comparatively high percentage of Serviceville and open country awareness of a single issue on the part of Protestants may be explained

TABLE 13. *Knowledge of Denominational Social Issue Statements in Per Cent for Selected Denominations—Main Town*

Church Membership of Respondent	N=	Response	
		No Knowledge	*Knowledge of at Least One Issue*
Baptist	43	81	19
Catholic	50	60	40
Christian	19	79	21
Congregational	71	85	15
Lutheran, Augustana	42	88	12
Lutheran, United	77	100	0
Methodist	80	67	33
Mission Covenant	54	78	22
Presbyterian	44	86	14
None	73	88	12

by the fact that each of these geographic areas included a substantial number of Mennonites, and without exception they were fully informed about the peace stand of their denomination.

Too much should not be made, perhaps, of the fact that the United Lutherans were uninformed about any stand of their denomination. This may represent an interesting phenomenon in itself. Only recently has this denomination developed a department for the purpose of interpreting the relevance of the gospel to specific social issues. It has long been zealous in theological interpretation. As an inheritor of the "two kingdoms" theory of Martin Luther, it was presumed that devoted and consecrated individuals would translate their devotion into responsible social action. That such is not the case without specific suggestion and help in discerning lines of application is now pretty commonly assumed. This particular denomination has been moving steadily out of its ethnic isolation and assuming a responsible and aggressive part in the total national life. As its constituents have moved into the main stream, they are developing participation patterns proportionate to those of other denominations. There is, for the time being, however, a difference. The old-line British-American denominations with Calvinistic background—Baptists, Disciples, Congregationalists, Methodists, and Presbyterians—belong in a tradition in which it was taken for granted that the active church participant assume responsibility for the life of the community as well. Those ethnic groups which came from a Lutheran tradition had no such background of presupposition and, in addition, were more likely to associate with one another because of language factor.

Unless one misreads the signs as indicated in this study and from any other sources, it may well be that as the Lutheran communicants lose their ethnic identification, while maintaining a strong disposition toward theological reasoning, they may evolve both a perspicacity and a high degree of involvement in social issues. These may even exceed those similar qualities among the inheritors of the Calvinistic tradition. The one apparent factor that may modify this prediction is the growing interest on the part of many in the Calvinistic tradition to reassess their own roots and rediscover the imperatives that lie within their own theological interpretation. Possibly another generation will be required before the full consequences of these trends become apparent.

Logic or common sense would seem to suggest that persons of above-average intelligence would probably be better informed than those of lesser competence. Actually the difference between the lowest and the highest divisions is only 15 per cent. Almost the same degree of difference prevails between the blue-collar and the white-collar categories. From these facts one is inclined to conclude that even among church constituents of superior ability there is not any great degree of interest in, or understanding of, the church's concern for the critical issues in society. One can but suspect that this fact is not wholly unrelated to the absence of any grounding in theological foundations or any awareness of the relevance of the Biblical record to contemporary problems.

LAYMEN, MINISTERS, AND SOCIAL ISSUES

It was thought that whatever might be the response of laymen to social issues, they might reveal something of their own attitudes by conveying the degree of their sanction of encouragement in these matters on the part of their minister or priest. The specific question was, Do you think your minister should be informed about such present-day problems as politics, race, the schools, U.S. foreign policy, etc.? The replies were almost never unambiguous. For the most part, ranging generally from 25 per cent to 50 per cent, the respondents indicated that the office carried with it the responsibility to be fully informed (Table 14). A significant number qualified their response in a way that might indicate lay resentment against implied superior knowledge. They contended that these are the sorts of issues on which everyone should be informed, not just the clergy. In the light of replies to the question about denominational positions on social issues, it is interesting that with the suggested references to politics, race, the schools, etc., these apparently did not serve as a reminder of any denominational emphases. This adds further evidence to the conclusion that denominational stands on these respective matters have gone unheeded.

There is no strong indication that laymen expect leadership from clergy for a better understanding of the relation between religion and society. As a matter of fact, one of the stock replies to the question about a minister's necessity for being informed on these matters was "Yes, he ought to be informed on them, but he ought not bring them into the pulpit." The reasons for this resentment against the minister's sharing his political and economic convictions, however theologically grounded, would itself make an interesting study. For the present it can only be deduced that: (1) the

TABLE 14. *Reasons Cited for Ministers' Knowledge About Social Issues in Per Cent for Selected Denominations—Main Town*

CHURCH MEMBERSHIP OF RESPONDENT	N=	REASONS CITED						
		Doctrinal						
		Two Worlds	Moral Principles Applicable to Society	Church Concerned with Society	*Office of Minister Requires Knowledge*	*All Should Be Informed*	*All Other*	*"Don't know"*
Baptist	44	18	2	5	64	27	16	7
Catholic	52	8	2	6	54	25	29	4
Christian	20	5	10	5	45	20	25	5
Congregational	41	10	20	2	22	15	32	15
Lutheran, Augustana	42	12	2	2	45	21	29	5
Lutheran, United	81	19	6	5	40	25	23	11
Methodist	53	17	11	2	32	15	32	11
Mission Covenant	54	15	11	9	41	17	24	2
Presbyterian	44	20	5	9	57	20	32	7
None	68	19	3	6	26	22	22	15

minister is no better informed than others; (2) religion and social issues should be kept separate; (3) the present equilibrium should not be disturbed by introducing extraneous elements, particularly in church.

The pattern that has now become rather familiar in Serviceville repeats itself. No one indicated that the priest need concern himself with these issues, and only 9 per cent thought laymen should be informed. Of the Protestants 32 per cent thought their clergy ought to be cognizant of the issues, while only 11 per cent felt the obligation applied to the laymen.

On the other hand, in the open country, 22 per cent of the Catholics felt their priests should be informed, and 57 per cent, the largest per cent registered anywhere, expressed the conviction that everyone should be possessed of such information. Among Protestants, likewise, the response for ministerial education and lay information stand out prominently.

Finally it is to be noted that almost three times as high a percentage of persons above average in intellectual ability wanted their clergy to be well informed as was the case with those who are classified below average. These results point to something that becomes increasingly clear throughout the study, namely, that ministering to individuals of widely varying intelligence makes necessary a type of ministry or training that is different from the usual pattern.

CHAPTER VIII

THE MINISTRY

No other professional role is being subjected to more redefinition than that of the ministry. This is true regardless of the type of community in which that ministry is provided. Some of the reasons are quite obvious, others obscure. One of them is the fact that now most communities have residents who are as well educated as the clergyman, so he no longer qualifies as the only intellectual leader. Often, too, by virtue of the fact that he is spokesman for, and primarily responsible to, only a limited segment of the community, he cannot command the widespread support received, for example, by the superintendent of schools or those in political office who experience a relationship with the whole local constituency. In addition there is the altered status of religion and religious institutions in a society that places high premium upon freedom from ecclesiastical and religious dictation. The minister no longer represents in himself or in his institution a force controlling community standards. Most important of all, however, is the uncertainty and confusion over the role of the church itself, the institution in which the clergyman performs his various functions.

All this and much more confronts both minister and laymen with uncertainties over any distinctive role the ministry fulfills in contemporary society. One thing, however, emerges as certain. The minister does stand as the central figure in the ecclesiastical scene. As the leader of a company of parishioners, he is asked to fill a role that he in part creates for himself. But also this role is created for him by the expectations of his parishioners and the total community of which he is a part. Actually his role may be vastly greater than either he or his parishioners are at present prepared to comprehend.

TOWN-COUNTRY FACTORS

This study is primarily concerned with the ministry in what are conventionally designated as town and country churches. However, size is not the determining factor in classifying a community. More important are the type of economy that dominates it and the way people earn their living.

The majority of all officially listed churches in the major denominations of the United States are in communities of less than ten thousand population. With the exception of those municipalities immediately adjacent to standard metropolitan areas, most communities of ten thousand or less are substantially influenced by their rural environs. Most of these communities and their churches have borne the stamp of rural influence. If to the number of those churches representing the major denominations were added the units of the various Pentecostal bodies and others that have recently come into increasing prominence, the majority figure would be even larger. Not all these units have full-time ministers, but each is served by an individual who is identified as a clergyman. It is a reasonable assumption that the largest percentage of ministers in this country is to be found in what are designated as town and country churches.

A strong case could be made for the fact that the most common conception of the minister's role comes from the traditional notions of the ministry as derived from experiences in the churches of town and country. This has led those who are responsible for this study to a limited examination of that role as understood by church and non-church members living in Corn County.

With the exception of River Town, all the churches of Corn County could be classed as town and country churches. This might be resented, understandably, by many of the Corn County churchgoers, particularly those of Main Town. Realistically, though, it must be recognized that even the churches of Main Town are composed of people who derive their living for the most part from the service of agriculture and from actual farming. Main Town with its six thousand population is, in the eyes of many of its residents, a small city. Nevertheless, if one uses the census designation of ten thousand for a community primarily related to agriculture as being still a rural community, Main Town would unquestionably qualify. A few observations concerning this classification of church may be pertinent to its present situation and the role of its leaders.

For a half century we have witnessed a growing concern for the town and country church. The year 1908 marked the beginning of the American Country Life Association, and in the same period there occurred the formation of a Town and Country Department in what was then the Federal Council of Churches. (Mark Rich, *The Rural Church*

Movement; Juniper Knoll Press, 1957.) Actually it was the apprehension over the deterioration and visible decline of the town and country church that accelerated the interest in country life in general, adding encouragement to the decision on the part of Theodore Roosevelt to create a commission for the purpose of coping with this unhappy situation.

In addition to the formation of an interdenominational department whose responsibility was to turn the tide of disintegration and decline in town and country churches, every major denomination developed a department of its own for the same end. One theory behind this widespread movement was the assumption that American life could be preserved at its best only if its rural roots were preserved. And the preservation of rural roots could be assured only if the rural church remained strong. There was enough truth in this theory to give it credence. What was happening to the town and country church, however, was emanating from outside the rural areas. Even though the quality of leadership enlisted for those churches was often of a superior quality and dedicated to the service of this particular type of church, the very best of leadership had to acknowledge that the illness was not something originating, or inherent, in town and country life itself.

Continuing even up to the present time much emphasis has been directed toward the recruiting and training of men and women for a specialized ministry in town and country churches. Recently there has been less tendency to magnify the importance of this particular type of church for its own sake and more inclination to stress the nature of the church itself, with special consideration for the peculiar responsibilities arising out of the type of community it serves.

Land-grant colleges with their vast resources in rural

sociology and technology gave unstintingly of their help to those who sought to strengthen the town and country church. However, it was not within their province to deal with the philosophical and theological problems involved in the massive cultural change that was engulfing America in particular and all the rest of the world as well.

Ministerial leaders equipped with understanding of the technological and social changes might help their congregations acclimatize and accommodate to the transition everywhere apparent—the larger farm units, increasing capitalization, co-operative purchasing and marketing, and increasing dependence upon resources from off the farm. But these movements and their implications could not be readily comprehended. Their meanings were not easily discernible.

The changes that have taken place in agriculture and industry are not to be met and dealt with by individual churches or denominations. They obviously represent forces as massive as our total society itself. Baffled by these forces, religious leaders concentrated increasingly on the problems of their own institution, the local church, supplemented by whatever co-operative action the ministerial association might engender through fraternal action.

As has been apparent from previous data reported in this study, church constituents are not particularly concerned with the wider and community aspects of their faith. After this situation was recognized, it was thought that it would be helpful to discern what functions actually are expected of chosen religious leaders.

QUALITIES DESIRED IN A MINISTER

The kind of replies given to an inquiry about the qualities and characteristics most sought in a minister might be of particular interest to young people considering full-time religious leadership. Perhaps the replies could indicate whether the historic function of the church as a place of both priestly and prophetic emphasis is being maintained. Other questions emerged. Is it possible, for example, that certain of the educational and prophetic functions of the church have passed into other hands—the school, the welfare agencies, political organizations and economic groups, and that the priestly function alone remains? Is this one of the interpretations to be drawn from the pronounced increase in liturgical life in practically all denominations? Or again, amid the swirl of vast forces, does the church provide for a measure of intimate and face-to-face relationships that serve to offset the impersonal forces that threaten inundation? Finally, is the professional leader one who can help people discern what is durable and permanent amid the change?

As was indicated earlier, church constituents in a previous generation often found it desirable to cross denominational lines for purposes of upward mobility. With social status more widely spread throughout the denominations and with the emergence of certain of the ethnic groups more fully into the American stream, the church fellowship has obviously served a purpose in facilitating this transition. Also, with each church having in its membership in varying degree some of the status figures of a community, and with a common assumption that each local church is or can become important in its community, the minister is evaluated for his contribution to this expectation. That church members of all denominations should, therefore, want their religious leaders to be capable of symbolizing the qualities on which society at large places its premiums is also readily understandable.

Alongside these overt and covert ambitions on the part of church members for their leaders there must be placed the kind of thinking that is currently going on in the ministry and among those preparing for it in theological training centers. All of this is inseparably related to the question of the nature of the church itself. No question is eliciting more diligent inquiry among thoughtful church leaders than this question of the nature of the church. The emergence of wholehearted co-operation on the part of all the major denominations as shown in the formation of the World Council of Churches within this generation gives evidence of what many church leaders have come to believe about the fundamental nature of the church.

The nature of the church determines the nature of the ministry. But irrespective of the unremittent and heart-searching study involved in attempting to discern the nature of the church, it has been almost exclusively conducted by the professional leadership. The church as an institution is taken for granted, and there is little, if any, questioning of its fundamental nature on the part of its constituents. It is understandable, therefore, that there should be uncertainty and confusion centering about the role of the church's leadership.

As a means of securing indications of the ministerial role, the question was asked, If you were a member of the committee looking for a new minister, what would you think were the most important qualities he should have?*

* Studies by many others have attempted to suggest a normative role for the ministry. Most recent of these is to be found in The Survey of Theological Education in the United States and Canada, conducted by H. Richard Niebuhr, in collaboration with Daniel D. Williams and James M. Gustafson, *The Purpose of the Church and Its Ministry* (Harper & Brothers, 1956). Samuel H. Blizzard conducted an analysis of the kinds and extent of work performed by ministers as revealed in

Some churches do not have the privilege of selecting a new minister, and this fact was frequently made plain. Some seemed to be relieved that they did not have to make the choice. Others felt that they could have done better than the ecclesiastical officials responsible for current appointments.

PERSONALITY

Outranking all other qualities in desirability is that of a good personality (Table 15). Even Catholics, for whom the personality of the priest is presumably secondary to his priestly functions, rate this quality highest. In fact in each of the four areas cited, the Catholics attach even more importance to the personality factor than do Protestants. Possibly the fact that the Mass and the ecclesiastical functions have not been subject to lay influence may accentuate the Catholic response to the personality of the priest himself. On this, at least, judgment can be exercised and expressed; whereas, in the priest's official functions, no adjustments have been thought possible.

Had the question been asked differently, less emphasis might have been placed on the personality aspect in the choice of a minister. The form that the question did take, however, enabled the respondents to make the response that was foremost in mind. If a series of choices had been offered and the respondent given opportunity to rate them, it is quite possible that one or more of the other responses might have taken precedence. It is significant that a good per-

---

a sample of the alumni of six representative theological seminaries. The director of that study has also undertaken, on behalf of the National Council of Churches, a study of laymen's opinions of the ministry. Our study, here recorded, seeks to present a limited but, we hope, helpful clue to the laymen's appraisal of the minister's role.

TABLE 15. *Qualities or Characteristics Expected of a Minister in Per Cent for Selected Denominations—Main Town*

CHURCH MEMBERSHIP OF RESPONDENT	N=	QUALITIES EXPECTED							
		Professional Qualities				*Personal Qualities*			*Other*
		Good Sermons	Good Education	Theological Ideas	Other	Good Personality	Exemplary Conduct	Other	
Baptist	43	35	19	9	63	54	12	42	30
Catholic	50	24	6	6	28	32	12	34	30
Christian	20	50	20	5	20	75	15	49	10
Congregational	71	54	16	6	47	51	13	58	13
Lutheran, Augustana	42	38	5	7	36	26	10	60	26
Lutheran, United	77	47	7	14	29	64	7	52	23
Methodist	80	56	5	15	39	71	26	46	15
Mission Covenant	54	46	9	17	63	46	2	41	24
Presbyterian	44	43	21	9	27	52	7	61	14
None	105	31	1	5	19	49	15	37	8

sonality, with whatever that implies, comes first to mind among the highest percentage of respondents.

In a society in which so high a premium is attached to "adjustment" and ability to get along with others, it is hardly to be wondered at that voluntary associations such as churches, which symbolize harmony in human relations, would desire as their leaders individuals capable of both symbolizing these qualities in themselves and fostering them among others. On the other hand lies the danger, if not the tragedy, of achieving harmony at the expense of integrity. There seems to be the beginning of a growing awareness that industry may have been paying too heavy a price for the absence of friction and the achievement of harmony at any cost. The wide acceptance accorded *The Organization Man,* by William H. Whyte, Jr., is an indication of this awakening.

Experts in maintaining harmony may serve to obscure the critical issues and keep the church on dead center impotent to exercise its reconstructive and creative role in the life of either individuals or society. Many thoughtful analysts of the church's role are asking whether the increase in the priestly functions are at the expense of the church's creative function. This is by no means to suggest that the priestly function is only that of minimizing conflict. Rightly conceived its function is to set individual and social conflict in their proper perspective and to enable the individual to deal constructively with conflict rather than merely to escape it.

Insistence on the possession of a good personality by the minister could also be another way of announcing that if what he represents is valid it ought to be reflected in the superior qualities of the religious leader himself. Whatever else religion is supposed to engender in the individual, it is a universal conviction that it should make for a well-balanced person—a wholeness that is characterized by stability. Since many of the respondents attempted to amplify what they meant by good personality, it seemed this was a part of what they were trying to say though articulation of this idea was understandably lacking. Hence, perhaps, the lumping together of so much under the category of good personality.

It is noteworthy that by far the highest percentage preferring good personality traits is found in the Methodist constituency in Main Town. This is the largest church in the community, with a broad range of economic and educational qualifications. As has been noted, it falls somewhat below the Congregational and Presbyterian churches in the percentage of high status constituents but probably reflects more nearly the national cross section of church participants. Good fellowship and broad participation in organizational life of this denomination are here reflected in the strong desire that its leadership symbolize these qualities prized so highly in the community at large. The respondents' references could likewise reflect the fact that the minister of this particular congregation has been permitted to remain as its leader for many years, and his wide acceptance both denominationally and locally may have served to influence the kind of reply they gave.

Less understandable, perhaps, is the fact that so large a percentage of United Lutherans also indicated that the personality of the leadership was of foremost importance. This is consistent with other replies of United Lutherans as has been noted earlier. For a church, however, that has been strongly liturgical and theologically minded, this high percentage (64 per cent) expressing first preference for a good personality may be further evidence that this denomination is now in its new relationship coming to resemble more nearly the pattern of other denominations. The Augustana Lutherans, on the other hand, are at the bottom of the list of those stressing the personality qualities of their spiritual leader. This again is consistent with previous documentation from this denomination. The Mission Covenant constituency, likewise of Swedish background, are considerably more interested in the personality of their leaders, ranking close alongside the Presbyterians and Congregationalists. Here again another denomination that has been moving rapidly into the main stream places high emphasis upon the same qualities as those denominations which have been permanently identified with the culture in which they live.

Next to the lowest in ranking personality as important is the Catholic constituency in Main Town. In each of the other communities, Catholics register greater interest in this characteristic. The reasons for this difference may be surmised but do not lend themselves to ready analysis.

Paralleling responses from Catholics living in the open country, they are close to the top in their insistence upon the good personality characteristic, perhaps reaffirming the independence and cultural similarity between Catholics in the open country and what seemed to be the pattern of other denominations.

Consistent with what has gone before is the fact that individuals of all levels of intellectual ability are alike in their emphasis on personality. Neither are the differences between men and women noteworthy in this regard, and only 10 per cent more of the white-collar workers indicated the importance of this quality than blue-collar workers.

SERMONS

Next in importance to personality is the desire for competence in the area that historically has been Protestant worship's most significant contribution—the sermon.

It could be conjectured that among Protestants, if a poll were taken, the outstanding single phase of the church's life would appear to be the preaching of the sermon. Generally speaking, if the sermon is good, the other components of the service of worship, even if less thought out and poorly executed, can be overlooked. On the other hand, no matter how excellently the total service of worship may seem to have been prepared, if the sermon is unsatisfactory, the congregation may register its disapproval of the entire service. There are some exceptions to this, of course, but apparently Corn Countians accept the tradition that preaching is the minister's most important single function. Actually nothing else comes even a close second. There were a good many suggestions that the minister ought to be diligent in parish visitation or have capacity for working with young people or old people, but these and other qualifications were not mentioned a sufficient number of times to make a distinct category for them.

Few attempted to spell out what constituted a good sermon. Of those who did, a small number volunteered the suggestion that the sermon should be Scripturally grounded. The number indicating that the sermon should interpret the meaning of the Christian faith for the major issues of the times was infinitesimal.

Traditionally, the sermon has been a means both of education and of inspiration—educational to the extent that the good news of the gospel is made plain and relevant for the life of the hearer, and inspirational in that it moves him to whatever action is required. As has already been made apparent, even the churches with the largest percentage of constituents endowed with superior intellectual ability seem not to possess any sturdiness of theological foundation that would undergird their appropriation of the good news. There may be an understandable correlation then between the uncertainty or indefiniteness about the nature of the sermon and the very low emphasis placed upon theological ideas as a qualification for religious leadership.

Preaching, the expounding of the church's message and the means of clarifying and expediting its mission, seems to be but slightly understood. Loyalty to the idea of the sermon as an integral part of church life in American religious culture may be noteworthy, but uncertainty over the function to be served by the sermon and the competence of the one presenting it has created a dilemma. The rising educational level of many congregations and the availability of excellent ideas through the various media of communication, if discretion is exercised, has created for the minister and preacher a new role which is perhaps not yet understood by the congregation nor fully accepted by the minister.

It is by no means certain that Corn Countians would respond enthusiastically to an interpreter of the gospel who possessed a skill for integrating the message with the total act of worship. Assembling for worship implies primarily a gathering to engage in traditional practices in company with one's neighbors rather than to attest in common to the glory of God and seek his guidance. Until this condition is changed there seems little likelihood that the position of the minister as a leader of worship will be enhanced and the uncertainty of the function of the worship service be modified.

OTHER QUALIFICATIONS

Too much importance should not be attached to the very few suggestions that the minister should be a person of good education. This may well have been taken for granted. On the other hand, it is noteworthy that it is the Presbyterian, Congregational, and American Baptist churches in Main Town that attach even a modest measure of importance to this criterion. Approximately 20 per cent of the respondents from these churches made mention of this characteristic. The next nearest was 9 per cent, and the others, all below that.

There is scarcely any difference between the respective appraisals of men and of women in regard to the "good sermons" qualification of the minister. And the range between the below-average respondent and the above-average respondent is only 12 per cent. Both seem to feel that the ability to deliver good sermons, whatever they are, is important. Between the blue-collar and the white-collar worker the difference is only 14 per cent.

Despite the uncertainties, and some negative implications from the data, one thing seems to be clear—that the people of Corn County are genuinely interested in the role of the minister. With the exception of one nonchurch member there was no hostility registered. On the contrary, the data would indicate, and the interviewers all reported, a warmth of response to the role these individuals were attempting to fill regardless of how well the role was qualified. A few respondents had had unfortunate experiences in their churches, but they were associated with specific individuals rather than with the profession itself.

In the sample for the interviews, several ministers were included. Each indicated that he regarded the entire scope of his relationships with the church members as his ministry, refusing to let the sermon carry the principal responsibility. In response to the question asked all the other respondents, that is, presuming himself to be a member of the pulpit committee, each minister placed individual integrity and sincerity foremost. No attempt was made to interview all the ministers, so this abbreviated report can only be in the nature of an unscientific postscript.

THE MINISTER'S CONDUCT

In the pretesting period for the study, questions were included dealing with the minister's use of tobacco, his appearing in informal dress, and his participation in social events of a "stag" nature. Both for reasons of brevity and because the responses had a great deal of similarity, it was finally decided simply to ask, Do you think a minister should conduct himself differently from other people in town?

The familiarity patterns of American social life, including the use of first names, have long since found their way into the life of many congregations. Business relations, fraternal organizations, professional groups, have fostered and encouraged the more intimate forms of address. Churches too have adopted this pattern in widespread fashion. Is not the church another voluntary association? So the theory runs, and its leader needs the assurance of the same warmth of fellowship that ostensibly marks all other voluntary associations.

Having already established the fact that most Corn Countians want their minister to be possessed of a good personality, and hence able to relate easily to all kinds and conditions of people, the question arises as to what extent his conduct shall resemble or differ from the rest of the community.

At this point, the evidence indicates, both churchgoers and nonchurchgoers desire that their minister or the ministry in general maintain a standard of personal conduct that is exemplary, whatever their own may be.

In Main Town, as Table 15 indicates, approximately three fourths of the respondents attest to their desire that the minister's conduct be such as to set an example for other people. To a lesser degree is this true in River Town and to a still lesser degree in Serviceville. On the other hand, in the open country this standard is most important of all. Among the Congregationalists and Presbyterians there is more disposition to disregard judgments toward the conduct of the pastor. The Methodists, on the other hand, who have resembled the latter two denominations in so many respects, make somewhat higher demands in the direction of the exemplary conduct of their pastor and are decidedly less inclined to be neutral. Women are inclined to ask more of their pastors by way of exemplary conduct than men. And the person of above-average intelligence is inclined to make this demand slightly stronger than the person of below-average intelligence. Again it is the churches of more pronounced ethnic background (Swedish) that register the very highest insistence upon the exemplary character of their religious leaders.

GENERAL OBSERVATIONS

Any value in the findings that pertain to qualities sought in the ministry lies more in what is omitted than in what is said. Lest more be implied than the comments convey, it must be added that the respondents were not asked to comment on the role of the minister as prophet or priest. That no one couched his responses in such terms is hardly surprising. It does seem significant that the qualities desired were only those which give superior status in a fraternal organization or a service club. The ability to preach a good sermon no doubt incorporates the assumptions of scholarship, delivery, and relevance. Even with making generous allowance that such was intended in the responses, there are still omissions in emphasis.

The almost total lack of theological structure revealed

throughout the study would indicate that the pew is not insistent upon a recognizable framework of thought. Theological depth on the part of religious leadership may be taken for granted by the pew, but apparently it makes no further demand and does not seek the results that theological depth might assure.

We recognize it is dangerous to generalize from such limited data. However, in view of the plight of the town and country church, described earlier, one can but conclude that the changes in agriculture are not wholly, and possibly not even mainly, responsible for the dilemma of the church in rural life. Until more is demanded of its leadership or its leaders create a demand for superior results, its standards will remain more nearly like those of other organizations in the community in which it is located.

It would appear that no sizable portion of the church membership has insisted on a demonstration of the gospel's inclusiveness, or else the ministerial leadership has been discouraged from pressing for it. The result is a limitation on the true role of the religious leader in his congregation and his community.

Both from the data and from wishful thinking one concludes that there is a distinctive and useful role for the religious leader in the types of communities studied. The role is not without a potential for greatness. The fact that the minister is held in such high esteem gives him great initial advantage. The restricted range of his activities may result from the circumscribed limits he has inadvertently accepted for himself, either by denominational exclusiveness or by a too limited conception of the role of the church.

CHAPTER IX

DENOMINATIONAL INFLUENCE ON PSYCHOLOGICAL CHARACTERISTICS

DENOMINATIONS HAVE, among their other functions, served the purpose of providing religious homes for people of the same ethnic group, that is, people of the same national background. Also they have maintained themselves as spiritual homes for individuals entertaining particular theological beliefs and religious practices. It has been noted that they also tend to serve the purpose of reinforcing the status structure of America and apparently of other nations as well.

If the Corn County analysis has validity, there is decreasing difference in the ideologies and belief structure of the various denominations. In their place is a uniformity of religious belief and practice fostered by the same forces that make for uniformity in the rest of American society.

Because of the sharp differences in ethnic background and in the original theological beliefs that characterized certain of the denominations, it was hypothesized that the adherents of the several denominational groups might reflect these differences in their own personality structures. There are many first-generation immigrants still in some of the churches of Corn County, and a large percentage of the total constituency of the county's churches are second- and third-generation descendants of immigrants.

The preceding chapters document the variations in general religious comprehension and in the respective interpretations of the ways these religious beliefs find expression in selected social issues. The phase of the study here described, however, seeks to ascertain more of the psychological structure of the various denominational adherents and also something of their intellectual and imaginative capacities. It was in this phase of the study that there were derived the various levels of intellectual ability that have been used in the reported findings in preceding chapters.

The psychological characteristics about which further evidence was desired are those which might result from a particular kind of religious experience or church background. In other words, did the type of denomination in which an individual was reared have a marked effect on his personality? For example, are Lutherans of Teutonic and Scandinavian background, products of catechetical training with positive and defined answers, any more likely to be rigid and subservient to discipline than those persons who have participated in a thoroughly permissive and what to some may seem a chaotic, theological training?* The areas of the psychic life of the interviewees which come under the general analysis of the study are:

* Attempts at this kind of analysis are not numerous. Ernst Troeltsch, in his *The Social Teaching of the Christian Churches*, attempts a sociological rather than a psychological appraisal but with theological overtones; H. Richard Niebuhr, in *Social Sources of Denominations*, made a unique contribution to this area. Robert Lee, in *The Social Sources of Church Unity*, has, likewise, made a recent and helpful addition to this field. Related indirectly, also, is Will Herberg's *Protestant-Catholic-Jew*, to which reference has been made earlier.

1. Family Emotional Attitudes
2. Peer Identification
3. Relationship to Authority
4. Sexual Adjustment
5. Basic Personality Pattern
6. Attitude to Inner Life
7. System of Inner Control
8. Intellectual Functioning
9. Imaginative Ability

The means used for analyzing the above phases of the individual psychic life are found in the Thematic Apperception Test. This test has come into increasing common usage because of its proven reliability and the relative ease with which it can be administered.*

The administration of the test consisted of showing the interviewees four pictures. Three of these are taken from the standard picture kit of the Henry A. Murray Thematic Apperception Test (Harvard University Press, 1943). The four pictures portray:

1. A young boy who is contemplating a violin that rests on a table in front of him. (Drawing by Christiana D. Morgan.)
2. A country scene: in the foreground is a young woman with books in her hand; in the background a man is working in the fields and an older woman is looking on. (Mural by Leon Kroll, reproduced by special permission of U.S. Department of Justice.)

* The report of this portion of the study relies heavily on the account of the Thematic Apperception Test as described by W. Widick Schroeder, Co-director of the project in his unpublished doctoral thesis "Religion in a Midwestern County."

3. A woman clutching the shoulders of a man whose face and body are averted as if he were trying to pull away from her. (Illustration by C. C. Beall.)
4. A woman and a baby lying on a bed with the woman looking at the infant. It was chosen primarily for its suggested religious significance. (Taken from Edward Steichen's Family of Man group exhibited in the Metropolitan Museum of Modern Art. Maco Magazine Corp., 1955.)

The interviewee was shown the sequence of pictures mentioned and asked to tell a story about each one, the story to have a beginning, a middle, and an end. The interviewer reported verbatim the observations made. In the narration of the story the interviewee revealed various recognizable and analyzable characteristics. A specialist in analyzing Thematic Apperception Tests was employed for the entire series of interviews, thus assuring a uniformity of interpretation. Obviously the Test is not one which can be interpreted by those without experience and training.

Much of the analysis must, of necessity, be quite technical. Below is a brief summary of the findings in each of the areas designated.*

FAMILY EMOTIONAL ATTITUDES

No significant differences between members of the various denominations are discernible. Where differences are observable they do not conform to preconceived notions or

* This part of the total study is voluminous and complex. Only the briefest summary of the findings is presented here, since any adequate report would require a fuller treatment than is consistent with the scope of this present volume. The more complete report will subsequently be made available.

hypotheses which might be drawn from observations about a particular denomination. It is concluded, therefore, that influences other than denominational affiliation are responsible for variations. Nor were there marked differences between sexes. The only significant differences appeared between those of high and low intellectual ability.

PEER IDENTIFICATION

Implied in this category is the capacity for relating to others who belong in the range of associates one might logically seek out for companionship. Report has already been made (Chapter IV) of the denominational affiliation of the friends of those interviewed. Peer identification reveals the measure of encouragement or inhibition which characterizes actual or potential association. The primary concern here, of course, is whether type of religious training may noticeably condition one's social relationships. The data indicates that denominational background has little if any bearing on peer relationships.

RELATIONSHIP TO AUTHORITY

The historic tie between religion and nationality has been fostered both by political-military leaders and by ecclesiastical authorities. Its usefulness in facilitating the objectives of both is commonly understood. In fact it was understood so well by the founding fathers of the United States that they wanted no part of it. A major objective of the liaison between these two forces in the life of a nation was designed to make for subservience to authority and to assure the minimum of defection from required thought and conduct.

Subservience or submission to authority is, however, not

the same thing as acceptance of authority. This whole area of psychological analysis is being regarded as a fruitful field for exploration particularly where voting prediction is sought or where new practices and innovations involving the public welfare and economic life are attempted.

Acceptance of authority and the absence of emotional turmoil in the face of authorized innovations may constitute one index of an individual's psychological well-being. Hence the interest in the possible role which religious background might play in predisposing a person toward one type of response or another. Again the data fails to sustain any hypothesis constructed around imputed differences. The slight difference between Catholics and Protestants cannot be accounted as significant. Nor were there important differences between denominations or between blue-collar and white-collar respondents.

SEXUAL ADJUSTMENT

Any assumptions that theological or denominational differences might be reflected in revelations of sexual adjustment are unfounded. Differences between Catholics and Protestants in the four geographic areas studied are negligible. Of the four areas, the open country respondents reveal a slightly higher percentage in the mature column for the over-all response and are slightly less inhibited, likewise.

Perhaps not wholly unexpected is the abnormally high percentage of those persons possessed of above-average ability who are judged mature in the matter of sexual adjustment (64 per cent), as contrasted with the 19 per cent of those thus rated in the below-average column. The below-average respondents are also substantially more inhibited and immature.

BASIC PERSONALITY PATTERN

All the other characteristics appraised under the Thematic Apperception Test are, of course, a part of the over-all psychological analysis. For purposes of the study, "Basic Personality Pattern" is included as a special category for the purpose of subsuming beneath it the general characteristics of assertiveness, passiveness, and hostility.

As the other psychological attitudes revealed no outstanding differences in the characteristics of persons who come from substantially different theological and ethnic backgrounds, it might well be surmised that no extraordinary differences would appear under the category of "Basic Personality Pattern." Such is the case. Assertiveness and passivity appear in approximately equal measure between Catholics and Protestants in the several communities.

Intellectual ability has been correlated with many other traits. It is, therefore, no surprise to discover that individuals possessed of intellectual ability above the average are recorded as possessing twice the measure of assertiveness as that which characterizes individuals of below-average intelligence.

ATTITUDE TO INNER LIFE

The profession of psychiatry has been built up around many of the psychological characteristics here reported, but of none is this more true than the attitude toward inner life. Do some religious traditions make for a ready acceptance of whatever mental attitude may prevail, perhaps justifying it on the Pauline tradition of being content with whatever state in which a person finds himself? Those individuals whose religious tradition has made them ill at ease with the tragedies of the world or the areas needing betterment have fostered a "divine discontent." In still others is the assumption that little can be done and that it is not man's role to rectify the ills of the world. But more than either of these forms of expression is the acknowledgment that there is no peace to be found in a state of rebellion.

Peace of mind in the form of acceptance is registered by approximately 60 per cent of all the respondents in each of the four geographic areas used in the study. Between the denominations there is only slight variation in the measure of acceptance.

SYSTEM OF INNER CONTROL

Much head wagging of recent years has accompanied expostulations deploring the loss of inner controls or stabilizers which were assumed to have been more prominently in evidence in preceding generations. (David Riesman, in *The Lonely Crowd,* has cited this as one of the phenomena attendant upon, and contributing to, the indecisiveness and lack of moral stamina in contemporary life.)

Briefly it can be stated that denominational background and the type of training afforded by the religious educational systems of the respective denominations made no particular difference. As between Catholics and Protestants and between the several communities, no significant differences are noticeable. On a train the author entered into conversation with a stranger who turned out to be chairman of the school board of a well-known suburb. He was lamenting the absence of inner control among the pupils of that school system. His solution was to introduce the rigid disciplines of certain parochial school systems whose virtues had appealed to him. This he would accomplish even at the violation of traditional church-state separation. Unfortunately, the data here available was unknown at the time or it might have been brought into the conversation.

Again the group above average in intellectual ability register twice the degree of flexibility as the below-average group and are approximately only one fifth as subject to the pressures from around them.

INTELLECTUAL FUNCTIONING AND IMAGINATIVE ABILITY

The type of message presented to a worshiping congregation or a study group, and the level at which it is presented, may make a substantial difference in the measure of comprehension with which the message is received. It has been one of the assumptions of this entire study that a rethinking of the level of presentation for the gospel message may be necessary if there is to be a fuller comprehension of its meaning. In our preaching we have taken for granted perhaps that there is a uniform level of comprehension and that the single presentation may be sufficient.

In each of the communities, and in the respective Catholic and Protestant divisions, there are a small number who qualify as "above average."

It is in the comparison of the denominations that a clue is reached which offers an explanation to some of the other data in the preceding portions of the study. For example, one denomination possesses the largest number of persons in the above-average category, but interestingly, the same denomination has almost the highest percentage of those with below-average capacity for intellectual functioning. This could account for some of the erratic response of this particular denomination in many of the preceding classifications. No one of the denominations has a significantly disproportionate number of the very capable or the less capable persons. Here again is cause to raise the question concerning fundamental differences, if any, between the respective denominations.

INTERPRETATION OF RELIGIOUS STIMULUS

Throughout the study no attempt has been made to define what is religious. Instead it has been taken for granted that participation in the various religious agencies and activities would in and of itself constitute a sufficient definition of what the participating individuals thought was religious. In the use of picture No. 4, attempt was made to ascertain levels of religious comprehension, that is, at what depth of feeling and understanding and articulation the respondent viewed the picture of the mother and baby. Some individuals, for example, saw this as simply a family scene. To others it was fraught with deep meaning involving the whole concept of creation, wonderment, and love.

Because there is a high degree of correlation between intellectual level and ability to articulate, it could be presumed that those who have imaginative capacities, depth of feeling, and superior ability to grasp relationships might be able to expound more comprehensively the story they saw in the picture. Replies from such persons were designated as "high" in the total range. Correspondingly, those who saw the scene without any particular meaning and described it thus would be rated "low."

The response of the three groupings ranged for intellectual ability is what might be expected—the persons of above-average intellectual ability are also the ones predominantly possessing unusual competence. Possibly the most significant findings in the data are those which reveal the comparatively small number of individuals in the churches who responded in a superior fashion.

Again, though the differences between denominations are not great, the range within each denomination is substantial. That blue-collar and white-collar workers do not necessarily differ in intellectual ability is further indicated by the fact that they are approximately equal in their responses.

In addition to the concern of this study for the spread of ability in a congregation, there is also a concern for that comparatively small group, present in every congregation but greater in some than others, for which it would appear that adequate provision is not being made. Whether they in any sizable number are more disaffected or maintain a larger measure of personal reservation about the usefulness of the church, this study cannot provide adequate information. It would appear, however, that they constitute a potential reservoir at present insufficiently utilized.

CHAPTER X

CONCLUSIONS FROM CORN COUNTY

THAT DENOMINATIONS ARE IMPORTANT in Corn County is undeniable. Why they are important is not so clear. The basis for observable differences between the constituents of the various denominations is less at the level of theological comprehension and ethnic-religious traditions than at economic levels. Also there is less difference in intellectual ability than in economic levels. It can be inferred from the general evidence that as denominations with specific ethnic backgrounds become full participants in the cultural activities of the majority, some of the differences that may once have characterized their members as participants in a particular denomination become less vivid and undistinguishable from those of the rest of their neighbors.

It becomes logical to ask, then, just what function the various denominations perform in present-day Corn County life. To answer this question fully would probably require the use of many subtle techniques. It will be recalled that the interviewees were not asked why they belong to a particular church but, rather, what it was that they liked best about their church. That the replies were almost wholly without any reference to ideological differences or characteristics would seem to give some validity to the suggestion that individual churches and possibly the denominations of which they are a part no longer serve to provide a home for those to whom particular creeds are important. Likewise, the survey of friendship patterns and the means of initiating those friendships would indicate that, whatever the bases may have been in a preceding generation, present-day friendships in communities such as those studied are not built predominantly upon denominational affiliations.

Compounding the evidence from all the areas of the study produces the conclusion that denominations serve a primary function other than that of increasing religious sensitivity. This is not to say that the churches perform a function other than the religious function but merely to assert that the divisions between the churches, important though they may be in the minds of their adherents and officials, no longer contribute anything distinctive to their members.

Parenthetically, it might be added at this point that while this writing was in process, the author spent an evening at a church meeting in a small town in the corn belt. Most of the membership was present and the purpose was to attempt again an affiliation with another denomination in the same small town. It was noted that the first attempt at this affiliation was made more than thirty years ago. Since that time five of the families represented in the meeting of this evening were now to be found in both denominations as a result of intermarriage. Social relationships were indistinguishable and many business activities were carried on in collaboration. Gingerly and reluctantly the group present admitted that there was no real basis for continuing the separation; but there was much feeling expressed to the effect that "the things we stand for" would be lost and "we would be swallowed up," because, assuredly, the other group would never accede to a genuinely co-operative arrangement. There was little discussion of the ultimate nature of the church and the possible increased likelihood of moving in the direction of that ultimate purpose under combined forces. The historical, the sociological, and the psychological elements were considerably more in evidence than the theological, which, it would be assumed, are of primary importance in the life of the church.

At the national and international level the ecumenical movement is thoroughly established and accepted. This is not to overlook tensions and very real problems which confront those working at the ecumenical level. It merely takes account of the fact that the ecumenical idea is accepted and applied by most of the major denominations. At the national and international level, ecumenism is grounded in theological comprehension and a growing concern to understand the nature of the church.

There is in Corn County an ecumenism also, but it is not informed by theological interests or a genuine concern to understand the nature of the church. Rather, it has been brought about by the necessity for collaboration and co-operation in community activities. Yet, significantly, only one per cent of those interviewed interpreted their participation in socioethical concerns on a theological or church-grounded basis. In fact, nothing in the entire study stands out more prominently than the absence of any theological grounding for the ongoing life of the church in its own organizational form and in its relationship to the community in which it is set.

Quickly have individuals who were confronted with such

a statement made reply that even though church people may not possess the theoretical and theological framework to interpret their interest in, and concern for, the society about them, the fact remains that they do participate and often carry very heavy burdens out of a genuine desire to serve their fellow men. And this they insist is due to their church affiliation and the kind of inspiration that has come from church participation. This cannot be denied. However, the further question has to be asked—whether it can always be assumed in the future that the basic intent of the life of the church will be given adequate expression in community life unless its people are familiar with the imperatives that lie within the faith. The Biblical illustration of apprehension over the fact that good works prescribed by the law were being done without sufficient grounding in faith is obviously applicable (Rom. 3:28; Gal. 3:11–12; James 2:26). Protesters are reprimanded and reminded that it is the doing of the good that is more important than merely having a suitable orthodoxy. One cannot but ask whether a generation that is unfamiliar with the Hebrew prophets, and their concern for the total community of which they were a part, can have confidence that prophetic traditions will play any part in social decisions and community welfare of the next generation.

The fact that each denomination presented a similar degree of unfamiliarity with the Biblical foundations and their relevance for the contemporary scene can but lead to the conclusion that (1) other forces have minimized, diluted, or rendered meaningless the Biblical insights as they pertain to society, or (2) ministerial leadership has been unwilling or unable to make clear the relationship between religious life and community responsibility as it is to be found throughout the records of the Hebrew-Christian history—or perhaps both.

As the record of Corn County and many others like it seems to suggest, the proliferation of denominations, which emerged as part of the various migrations earlier referred to, fractured the single cultural emphasis that prevailed during the earliest period of Corn County settlement. There is no reason to assume that the emergence of industrialization in the nation at large and the impact of technological society in the realm of agriculture would not have done exactly the same thing. Actually all of the adherents of the various denominations have adopted the technological advancements in agriculture with almost equal rapidity. For a brief time the Mennonites resisted automobiles and tractors, but to stay competitive in a highly commercialized agriculture they quickly conceded to the advancing technology and are now able to hold their own and possess a measure of prosperity in some instances even in excess of their contemporaries. It would appear that the technological revolution in agriculture, and the corresponding development of organizations and community life that have resulted therefrom, has been more influential in making for community cooperation than has any Christian doctrine of community which may lie within the heart of the message of the several denominations.

THE MINISTRY

Professional religious leadership, in the minds of the parishioners, fulfills common objectives, and the qualities desired in them are very much alike regardless of the denomination represented by the parishioners. This is the evidence presented by all of the denominations here reported and from some others not included in the tabulation because of insufficient number in the sample. (This would include Episcopalians, Mennonites, Pentecostals, Jehovah's Witnesses, and various smaller sects.) An inquiry of the professional leadership itself was not conducted because of several other exhaustive studies of this problem. (See footnote, pp. 129–130.) Had the ministers been questioned as a separate professional group, some unique and perhaps quite different responses might have been secured. In this study, however, we are judging the results of ministerial leadership only by what their laymen seem to understand the minister's role to be, based upon acquaintance with ministers of other denominations as well as their own.

That there was almost no mention of the teaching function of the ministry and its capacity for leadership in a fuller comprehension of the meaning of the faith which the church espouses would seem to be of some importance. It may well be that the ministers in any number of the churches represented might regard this function as among their most important. If one can judge by an initial and perhaps spontaneous response to the query asked of the laymen, no one seemed to put this skill or capacity high on the list.

Capacity for good preaching was frequently mentioned, but upon request to expand that idea few could do so except by a rephrasing of the idea itself. What constitutes good preaching, aside from insistence that it be Scripturally grounded, is not something about which church people could be very explicit or articulate. The almost universal concern about the function and value of the sermon, and preaching in general, is apparently mirrored in the attitude of Corn Countians toward this important part of the church's life.

Despite this seeming criticism of the minister as teacher and preacher through the medium of the sermon, the criticism can in no wise be construed as disaffection or hostility toward preaching as a part of the church's life. The sermon is taken for granted. Some ministers apparently are "good at it," whereas others present something which at least is not resented and may actually give the listener a feeling of righteousness for having sat through the time of the sermon without visible protest. But traditionally has not the sermon been the high point of much of Protestant worship in which the worshiper is both inspired and enlightened? A high school student once gave in the presence of the author what seems a creditable definition of a good sermon. "It should tell you something you didn't know before, it should be related to the Bible, and it should make you want to be better." No doubt many of the sermons of Corn County pastors fulfill all three of those criteria. If the role of the minister is that of interpreter of God's Word to the present time and if he is the one capable of inspiring worshipers to yield themselves to the ways of God as known in Jesus Christ, might it not be assumed that such a function would have been understood and appreciated by at least a fair number of devoted church people, perhaps the 30 to 40 per cent who indicated consistent church attendance?

Preaching may not be for some religious leaders, however, the place in the total professional life where they make their greatest contribution. The life of the church is the life of worship and of service. These two facets are inseparable and neither can exist in genuine form very long without the other. Why no one mentioned worship and the capacity for leadership in this important phase of the church's life may not constitute a mystery, but it is something of a disappointment. Even the denominations that have placed the greatest amount of emphasis on the discipline of worship in their public services of worship make no mention of the ability to lead in worship in the selection of a minister. It was indicated earlier that the denominations emphasizing what is called a more liturgical form of worship seem to produce in their constitutents no more familiarity with either theological framework or social expression than those denominations whose primary emphasis has been less formal.

Roughly it can be assumed that worship takes place on two levels: (1) the habitual and (2) participation with full intellectual response. In Corn County churches, some 25 per cent of the membership could be classed as above average in intellectual ability, but even these persons indicate no particular desire for a ministry that makes worship intellectually meaningful. The impression is given that the participants in public worship are auditors and that they do not regard it as a function of their spiritual leader to engage them in conscious participation as worshipers.

It can only be concluded that unawareness of the meaning and the purpose of public and private worship is closely related to the inability to express the relation between faith and action or between one's church and public responsibility. This relationship has obviously not been made clear. This may or may not be the fault of the minister—he may have attempted it and found his interpretations unacceptable, or the ears of his hearers stopped, or that the seed fell on hard ground.

If the minister's first task is to interpret the ways of God to man and to lead men into the fuller understanding of God's ways, he must, presumably, be one who is aware of the events and conditions of his own time. His people have the right to expect from him a clarification of contemporary events in the light of historical criteria, particularly the criteria found within the Biblical record.

To ask of the ministry that it be expert in all phases of our complex society is asking more of it than any one profession or one individual is capable of producing. Since the days when the minister was *the* person in the community, a high degree of specialization in the role of interpreters of contemporary society has been made necessary. The observations of the political scientist and the historian, to say nothing of the polls analyst, are increasingly sought. Social psychologists and social anthropologists perform unique functions in analyzing the ways of men, in both modern and primitive societies. The minister cannot, of course, be all these things. He must, however, be sufficiently acquainted with what contemporary man's experience is doing to him as a person to be able to appraise judiciously the fulfillment or distortion of man's destiny as seen from a theological perspective. This, at least, the congregation has the right to expect. The minister may differ from the pollster and the international relations expert, or on the other hand he may thoroughly agree with them, but in either event he does so from foundations and norms whose validity is well grounded.

A ministry preoccupied with denominational competition or focusing on the minutiae of a limited perspective can hardly provide the long-range vision expected of the people of God. The tasks demanded of the clergyman acting as personnel manager for a local congregation may obscure the ultimate objectives of the church itself. This seems to have occurred in so large a measure that congregations simply do not expect their religious leader to provide guidance at that level.

Another even more demanding task that influences the minister's primary work is the large measure of attention necessitated by pressure from groups specializing in "fellowship." It is assumed by many that the church must emulate the patterns of other voluntary associations in order to "get ahead." Through such pressures as this, a high premium is placed upon "being a good mixer," as the interviewing indicated. How many ministers have wished their men's clubs might grapple with the real issues around them, and perhaps even with the problems related to man's ultimate nature and destiny. Instead they must settle for a travelogue on Yucatán or Sitka.

Visitors from abroad are amazed at the percentage of Americans who attend church with regularity. It is apparent that this regularity is not due primarily to any persistent desire for a clarification of the role of the individual or a spiritual interpretation of society or of the meaning of life itself. Whatever it is that institutional church life provides, it is somehow related to the life and work of the one who is employed to give leadership to the institution of the church. It would appear that the ministry has accommodated itself to that undefined but nonetheless realistic role. The role as understood by the laymen has thus become the role accepted by the religious leader himself. Since it is assumed that no very great special qualifications are required to fulfill the role as unconsciously defined by the laymen, no more is asked of him by way of intellectual leadership.

There is no little resentment among Corn County people that they are unable to secure as their pastors some of the young men of unusual promise. These men seem to be drawn instead to communities bursting with new homes and Sunday schools whose potential membership alone is greater than the combined membership of a half dozen Corn

County churches. The interesting thing is that, despite this fact, some uncommonly able men have consented to serve Corn County churches, and often at a scale of remuneration lower than would be available to them in metropolitan centers. A suggestion that several churches of a given community unite to secure more adequate leadership and a more balanced program for the religious education of their children is not seriously considered. It is more desirable to maintain the struggling denominational units than to travel a few extra miles for a combined program in their own denomination or suffer the break with history which a co-operative church experience would seemingly necessitate. Trained leadership is less necessary, apparently, than the retention of a tradition.

One eventually comes to the conclusion that it is not merely the tradition to which individuals cling but perhaps to the fear of change and innovation that might be necessary under competent and imaginative leadership. Conversation with some of the ablest of the Corn County ministers bears out this thesis. A frustration mounting at times to desperation is revealed by some of the more dedicated and highly intelligent ministers. They provide a clue to the reason why so few outstanding young people from Corn County want to train for the ministry of the kinds of churches they know in their home communities.

Obviously, young people are not inspired to enlist in a caretaker operation. The disinterest in the realm of ideas, as evidenced by the lack of information in matters relating faith to society and of faith to the meaning of existence, creates the assumption that no major advances are being made on intellectual frontiers.

For our own period of history, it is assumed that the major advances are in the realm of science. Thoughtful interpreters recognize that even more important is the function and direction of science. This poses philosophical and theological problems. It is with such problems as these that the church presumably is involved if it fulfills its purpose. It would be hard to imagine a congregation in Corn County that would encourage this kind of exploration, even though it would appear to be a major responsibility of the church.

As has been suggested earlier, Corn County is a large-scale beneficiary of the technological and economic revolution. To the great credit of the ministerial association it can be reported that the members instigated a forum dealing with the implications of this revolution for agriculture. They brought to the county some able interpreters in a series open to the entire community on behalf of the co-operating churches. There was a modest response.

A review of the leadership list of the constructive movements and organizations in Corn County reveals a repetition of the same names. They are the names of persons in the superior intellectual ability group, and to borrow a phrase from another era of agriculture, "they are the willing horses who are often sorely overworked." Might not one of the functions of religious leadership be that of interpreting with greater clarity the role of public duty and community service both for those who are already overworked and for those who have not as yet comprehended the relation between faith and responsibility? In this fashion, might not the minister amplify his own usefulness and magnify the functions of the institution he leads? In all probability not every clergyman in every church is capable of performing this function. Co-operatively, however, resources can be secured to do for a special group across denominational lines what no one group is able to do for itself.

No single role of the ministry has come into greater prominence in the past quarter century than the role of the minister as counselor. All the major theological seminaries have made a place for instruction in counseling and interpersonal relations. Major changes in social structures heightening the sense of instability place increasingly heavy strain upon the personal lives of everyone. This fact in itself may account for some of the undefinable importance of the church as an institution, despite the indefiniteness of the reasons for adherence to it. But more than that is the fact that the increase of total insecurity has confronted its victims with the longing to turn somewhere for needed guidance.

For many who are caught in circumstances beyond their control, either economic or emotional, the trained welfare worker provides help and guidance. But many of the problems confronting those in distress or uncertainty are rooted in what may be basically theological or philosophical issues. They are in some degree the product of the value system of the troubled individual.

Whether the problem is that of tangible assistance, acquainting the person with available resources—material or psychological—or whether the issue is fundamentally one of life's meaning and values, the minister, it is increasingly recognized, is one to whom it ought to be possible to turn with confidence. The kind of training being made available in theological seminaries, and for men already active in the ministry, through programs related to mental hospitals or to psychological and psychiatric departments of general hospitals is equipping ministers for this service.

Despite the historic function of counselor and guide, which the ministry represents, only a very small fraction of the people of Corn County indicated they had consulted their minister on personal problems. This may come as something of a surprise to the ministers themselves who seem to be constantly occupied with such problems as family difficulties, placement of the aged, hospital calls, and assisting in legal matters in and out of courts. Actually, the small percentage relying upon the ministry for counsel may not give a fair picture of the aid available. The mutual aid system, historically identified with rural living, has not wholly disappeared. In small communities people do still know about the needs of, and assume responsibility for, their neighbors. Also, welfare agencies have become an acceptable part of the total rural pattern.

However, the disinclination to consult the clergyman may also stem from something inherent in the very nature of the small community itself. It may be easier to consult a clergyman in the anonymity of the city than in a community where personal relationships are more commonly known. In the small congregation, which characterizes most of the churches of Corn County, there is a heightened embarrassment due to having one's own problem occupy so large a proportion of the minister's attention, regardless of how skilled a counselor he may be. It must be quickly added, however, that there are instances of such devoted leadership with capacity for trust that the size of the congregation has not invariably been a deterrent to a valued counseling relationship. It would seem that the weight of the evidence, nevertheless, is on the side which suggests that more adequate church units with qualified leadership might make a significant addition to the service of the church in Corn County.

THE CHURCH AND COMMUNITY

The term "community" is here used, not in its geographic sense, but rather with reference to the theological meaning of the term. In so many facets of the study it has been apparent that social and psychological characteristics have taken precedence over theological imperatives. Among the most obvious facts here documented is the division of church groups according to intellectual ability and social status. There is some evidence that the open society imputedly characteristic of this country is effecting a realignment or an equalizing of privilege and status across the various denominations. Illustrative of this on a national level is the now-familiar pattern of Pentecostal groups and others, but recently accorded sectarian status, now building substantial pseudo-Gothic edifices. In Main Town when the United Lutherans built a beautiful modern structure on the edge of the town, their former sanctuary was purchased by an upward mobile Pentecostal congregation.

Despite the realignment and upward mobility within denominations, the several denominations maintain in the popular opinion a status significance For the present at least there are noticeable differences in the ratio of membership by economic status and intellectual ability, consciously or unconsciously. The churches, it would seem, have become class selective.

Of some significance is the fact that increasingly church members are finding their friendship patterns and associations outside their own denominational range but still within their own intellectual level and social rank. This would seem to bode well for the diminution of artificial denominational barriers. It still leaves, however, the economic and social strata more or less intact across denominational lines and identifying the various institutions. Wittingly or unwittingly, the one organization and institution dedicated to the fact of man's equality before God serves to foster division and difference in the life of the community—the geographic community.

Few subjects are as delicate as that which realistically confronts the differences in a community, differences based on position and status. Again, in an open society with constant movement across class lines and the magnification of status being fostered by business associations and the society columns of the press, it would be strange if these divisions did not find their parallels in all forms of social life. Attention is called to this phenomenon here, however, not merely to take cognizance of its existence, as the study would seem to indicate, but to query whether the fuller comprehension of the nature and meaning of the church itself on the part of those capable of grasping such ideas might serve to minimize tensions and differences in the life of the local community. In other words, may not a genuine confrontation of the meaning of the church serve to evaluate the life of the sociological community over against the standards of the theological concept of community?

APPLICABILITY TO OTHER GEOGRAPHIC AREAS

Readers who are familiar with the corn belt will note that the denominational representation of Corn County is not identical with certain counties they know. There are some counties that would be overwhelmingly dominated by a single denomination. There are others that would have a very high representation of church groups only slightly represented in Corn County. Obviously, then, the representation of denominations in Corn County cannot be said to represent fairly every county in the region. This would certainly be true. However, even under the danger of claiming more for the study than is warranted, it would be our guess that the findings reported here would not differ greatly from those which would be secured using a similar interviewing process in the other county or counties.

In Chapter I it was suggested that Corn County is typical of most, if not all, of the counties of the corn belt. On the strength of this fact we have been bold to suggest that the observations here made are applicable to much of the entire area. The pitfall of claiming more for a study than the facts warrant is one of the easiest into which to stumble. To be absolutely accurate one would of course have to make an identical study of the other 468 counties. It is the virtue of a sampling process that a 100 per cent "universe" is unnecessary when a reliable sample has been used. Our justification in claiming typicality for Corn County lies in its similarity both to many other counties of the region and to a reasonable familiarity with the region itself. Thus it is concluded that the limited findings here reported are probably a fair representation of what would be found throughout the region.

It will be quickly noted that Corn County is situated in an area of relatively high prosperity. When statements are made describing the sad state of the farmer there is usually a modification concerning those areas where mechanization has been carried farthest and where the farm units are large enough to compete successfully. Though there is not uniform prosperity in the corn belt it is, generally speaking, an area of relative agricultural prosperity. Both farmers and those inhabitants whose livelihood depend upon agriculture have experienced a measure of security in excess of some of the areas requiring less mechanization or capital investment per producing unit.

Basically, the conditions prevailing in Corn County do not

differ materially from those characterizing areas wherein other types of agriculture predominate. The technological process in agriculture has blanketed all the major producing areas of the nation. It is the hypothesis of the study that it is in a large measure the mechanization and technical advances made by agriculture which have so largely conditioned the life and thought of people living in agricultural regions. Their response to the message of the gospel and the work of their churches is determined by their unconscious involvement in this technological-commercial culture.

Thus with the exception of some minor differences it is hypothesized that this analysis and description could be applicable to counties titled Wheat County, Dairy County, Fruit County, Vegetable County, or Range Livestock County. There seems less likelihood that it would apply to the cotton-producing areas, or to those producing tobacco. Of this we would prefer to have judgment from persons better acquainted with those regions.

Though Corn County derives its major income from agriculture, its economy is inseparably identified with that of urban society, and its ways are often undistinguishable from those of urban life. Another way of saying the same thing is to assert that urban life in America has influenced and colored a large part of what, less than a century ago, could be readily identified as rural. From this can be deduced what common-sense observation has long since concluded—that the opinions, reactions, and thought processes of urban people and those in areas of commercial agriculture are in many respects similar. No study comparable to this one has been made in a metropolitan area. Those conducting the study here reported are, and have been, residents in both rural areas and metropolitan centers. Acquaintance with urban and suburban churches and their people prompt the generalization and hypothesis that the findings from Corn County would in most respects be paralleled in an urban setting. It is our belief that the same deficiencies in the belief structure which appear so prominently and frequently in Corn County would also be markedly apparent in Boston and Seattle, and cities in between. In other words, we suspect the conditions revealed here are a national phenomenon related to our commercial-industrial, technological culture.

Behind the undertaking of this study, therefore, is not simply a desire to document some facts concerning religious life in any particular region. The impelling motive was to gain a more accurate picture of contemporary religious life in the United States. A large amount of theorizing has been undertaken relative to the so-called religious revival of the mid-twentieth century. This phenomenon has become both the whipping boy and the symbol of hope for interpreters of religion in our culture. It was believed necessary that a more accurate picture be acquired of the background against which any alleged revival is being or might be experienced.

It is not within the scope of the present analysis to suggest more desirable alternatives and the means of their accomplishment. That the authors of the study are not happy with the findings may be apparent in the very undertaking and the hypotheses with which it began. Many generalizations about contemporary religious life in America have been made on the basis of personal experience and with varying degrees of perceptivity. This study attempts to utilize empirical data as a basis for some reasonably accurate observations. The data itself does not carry within it the means of its reversal, if it should be deemed unsatisfactory. That responsibility rests with the persons who may not be content with the findings here reported.

If this study serves to add any stimulus toward strengthening the role of the church in our society, its purpose will have been accomplished.

INDEX